4 50

113 208

D1369078

Larkin

Open Guides to Literature

Series Editor: Graham Martin (Professor of Literature, The Open University)

Current titles

Angus Calder: Byron
Walford Davies: Dylan Thomas
Roger Day: Larkin
P. N. Furbank: Pound
Graham Holderness: *Women in Love*
Graham Holderness: *Wuthering Heights*
Jeannette King: *Jane Eyre*
Graham Martin: *Great Expectations*
Roderick Watson: MacDiarmid

Titles in preparation

Pieter Bekker: *Ulysses*
Dinah Birch: Browning
Jenni Calder: *Animal Farm* and *1984*
Peter Faulkner: Yeats
Anthony Fothergill: *Heart of Darkness*
Brean Hammond: *Gulliver's Travels*
Graham Holderness: *Hamlet*
Graham Martin: *The Prelude*
Bob Owens: *Robinson Crusoe*
David Pirie: Shelley
Jeremy Tambling: What Is Literary Language?
Ron Tamplin: Heaney
Dennis Walder: Hughes
Ruth Whittaker: *Tristram Shandy*

Philip Larkin (©1984 Byrnmor Jones Library, University of Hull).

ROGER DAY

Larkin

Open University Press
Milton Keynes · Philadelphia

Open University Press
Open University Educational Enterprises Limited
12 Cofferidge Close
Stony Stratford
Milton Keynes MK11 1BY, England

and
242 Cherry Street
Philadelphia, PA 19106, USA

First Published 1987

British Library Cataloguing in Publication Data

Day, Roger, *1945–*
    Larkin.—(Open guides to literature).
    1. Larkin, Philip—Criticism and
    interpretation
    I. Title
    821'.914   PR6023.A66Z/

ISBN 0 335 15093 4
ISBN 0 335 15084 5 Pbk

Library of Congress Cataloging in Publication Data
Main entry under title:

Day, Roger, *1945–*

        (Open guides to literature)

        1. Larkin, Philip,
    I. Title   II. Series.
    PR6023.A66Z

ISBN 0 335 15093 4
ISBN 0 335 15084 5 (pbk.)

Text design by Clarke Williams
Typeset by Quadra Associates Ltd, Oxford
Printed in Great Britain by J. W. Arrowsmith Ltd, Bristol

Contents

Series Editor's Preface

The intention of this series is to provide short introductory books about major writers, texts, and literary concepts for students of courses in Higher Education which substantially or wholly involve the study of Literature.

The series adopts a pedagogic approach and style similar to that of Open University Material for Literature courses. *Open Guides* aim to inculcate the reading 'skills' which many introductory books in the field tend, mistakenly, to assume that the reader already possesses. They are, in this sense, 'teacherly' texts, planned and written in a manner which will develop in the reader the confidence to undertake further independent study of the topic. They are 'open' in two senses. First, they offer a three-way tutorial exchange between the writer of the *Guide*, the text or texts in question, and the reader. They invite readers to join in an exploratory discussion of texts, concentrating on their key aspects and on the main problems which readers, coming to the texts for the first time, are likely to encounter. The flow of a *Guide* 'discourse' is established by putting questions for the reader to follow up in a tentative and searching spirit, guided by the writer's comments, but not dominated by an over-arching and single-mindedly-pursued argument or evaluation, which itself requires to be 'read'.

Guides are also 'open' in a second sense. They assume that literary texts are 'plural', that there is no end to interpretation, and that it is for the reader to undertake the pleasurable task of discovering meaning and value in such texts. *Guides* seek to provide, in compact form, such relevant biographical, historical and cultural information as bears upon the reading of the text, and they point the reader to a selection of the best available critical discussions of it. They are not in themselves concerned to propose, or to counter, particular readings of the texts, but rather to put *Guide* readers in a position to do that for themselves. Experienced travellers learn to dispense with guides, and so it should be for readers of this series.

This *Guide* will be most usefully studied in conjunction with *The North Ship* (2nd edition, Faber, 1966), *Jill* (2nd edition, Faber, 1964), *A Girl in Winter* (Faber, 1947), *The Less Deceived* (The Marvell Press, 1955), *The Whitsun Weddings* (Faber 1964), and *High Windows* (Faber 1974). They are all available in paperback editions.

Acknowledgements

My thanks go to the Open University for permission to develop this book from material originally contributed to their course on twentieth-century poetry, and especially to Graham Martin for his help and many suggestions during the course of its composition. I am grateful, too, to the secretaries of the Faculty of Arts for their patient work in putting the typescript through the word-processor.

Grateful acknowledgement is also made to: Kingsley Amis, for permission to quote from 'A Bookshop Idyll' (copyright 1956 Kinglsey Amis. Reprinted by permission of Jonathan Clowes Ltd., London, on behalf of Kingsley Amis); the estate of Philip Larkin, and the BBC for permission to quote from the radio programme 'Philip Larkin talks to A. N. Wilson'; the estate of Philip Larkin and the BBC for permission to quote from the television programme 'Monitor'; the BBC for permission to quote from the radio programme 'Something to be Said'; Faber & Faber Ltd and the Overlook Press for permission to quote from *Jill* and *A Girl in Winter*; Faber & Faber Ltd for permission to quote from *The North Ship*, *The Whitsun Weddings*, *High Windows*, *Required Writing* and W. H. Auden's *Collected Shorter Poems*; London Weekend Television Ltd for permission to quote from the 'South Bank Show: Philip Larkin' (1982); the University of Hull for permission to use the portrait of Larkin taken by their photographer, Alan Marshall. Excerpts from 'The Building' 'Show Saturday' 'To the Sea' 'The Card-Players' 'Annus Mirabilis' 'Going Going' 'The Old Fools' 'Sad Steps' and 'High Windows' in HIGH WINDOWS by Philip Larkin. Copyright © 1974 by Philip Larkin are reprinted by permission of Farrar, Straus and Giroux Inc. and Faber and Faber Ltd. Quotations from 'At Grass' 'Myxomatosis' 'Next, Please' 'No Road' 'Wants' 'Reasons for Attendance' 'Maiden Name' 'Poetry of Departures' 'Coming' 'Church Going' and 'Absences' are reprinted from *The Less Deceived* by permission of the Marvell Press, England. The extract from 'Aubade', which first appeared in the *Times Literary Supplement* (23 December 1977) appears with the permission of the estate of Philip Larkin and Faber and Faber Ltd.

1. Larkin's Early Life and Career

Philip Larkin was born in Coventry in 1922, the second child in a middle-class family. He attended the King Henry VIII School there until he was eighteen and remembers his childhood as being 'all very normal: I had friends whom I played football and cricket with and Hornby trains and so forth.'[1] He spent a lot of time reading, especially in the Sixth Form when he recalls concentrating 'on English which was the only thing I really had any instinct for'.[2] In this it was likely that his father was a considerable influence for, according to a friend at the time, Sydney Larkin (who was the City Treasurer) 'had a great love of English Literature, and especially of D. H. Lawrence, and he enjoyed poring over dictionaries, Fowler and Ivor Brown.'[3] Larkin's command of the English language and his occasional use of the unusual word perhaps had their origin here. He began to write at about the age of sixteen and recalls that 'the first poem I ever wrote was set for homework. We had to write one, about anything. We were all absolutely baffled and consternation reigned.'[4] What started as a task soon became a form of hobby for he began to write 'ceaselessly . . . now verse, which I sewed up into little books, now prose, a thousand words a night after homework'.[5]

In 1940, Larkin went to St John's College, Oxford. Having failed a medical examination for the Army because of poor eyesight, he was able, unusually at the time, to complete a full three years. He also suffered from a bad stammer until he was twenty-one. Such handicaps perhaps contributed to what was to prove a somewhat sombre view of life. At Oxford, he chose to read for a degree in English Literature and Language. He 'soon had several circles of friends at Oxford – the college circle, the jazz circle, possibly the literary circle.'[6] 'To outward view,' writes his friend Kingsley Amis, 'Philip was an almost aggressively normal undergraduate of the non-highbrow sort' and, in spite of what appears to have been a pretty general disparagement for much of the syllabus[7], Larkin took a First Class degree in 1943. His first poem to be published appeared at this time in *The Listener* and others followed in undergraduate magazines. Kingsley Amis (to whom Larkin later dedicated *XX Poems*) recalls that 'parts of *Jill* were already in existence' at this time, 'for at that stage of his life his main intention was to become a novelist'.[8]

In 1943, Larkin left Oxford and returned home where, while writing *Jill*, he received an enquiry from the Ministry of Labour as to whether he was employed. The unstated implication was that he might be allocated to work of national value in time of war. Thus prompted, he applied for and was appointed as Librarian in Wellington, Shropshire where he remained for three years. He arrived there more by accident than design as it was the first job he had applied for. He later reflected of this period that, 'feeling strange and being away from friends and home and so on, I think it did create a raw state of mind which was all very fruitful'.[9] It is not surprising, then, to learn that during these years he wrote 'continuously as never before or since.'[10] He was concentrating on fiction and, according to his own sombrely amusing account of those years, he finished *Jill* and began a second novel.[11] He was also writing poems, some of which were published in 1944 in a volume entitled *Poetry from Oxford in Wartime*. These poems appeared again the following year with others in Larkin's first individual collection, *The North Ship*, published by the Fortune Press at a price of six shillings (1945). His novel *Jill* (reflecting aspects of life in the Oxford of wartime where it had been begun) was published in 1946 and it was followed in 1947 by *A Girl in Winter* which draws on his experience as a librarian. By the time his second novel appeared, Larkin had moved to a new post as Assistant Librarian at University College, Leicester where he continued to study in his spare time for professional qualifications, eventually acquired in 1949. He has since recalled how 'between 1945 and 1950 I strove to write novels, many different novels, and they all failed. It had just gone.'[12] Kingsley Amis, too, recalls that considerable progress had been made on a third novel, a 'serio-comic account of the gradual involvement of a rising young executive in the motor industry, Sam Wagstaff, with a working-class girl he knocks down in his car coming home from the factory'. There were plans, too, for a fourth novel which was to be a saga involving many people's lives.[13] Amis's explanation for the abandonment of the third novel, as of the plans for its 'more ambitious successor' is 'fear of failure'.[14] Larkin's own explanation was that 'my novels really weren't novels, they were poems, long, diffuse poems, perhaps.'[15]

In October 1950, Larkin moved from Leicester to become one of the two sub-librarians at Queen's University, Belfast, where he stayed until March 1955 when he went to the University of Hull as Librarian. Both the place and job seem to have suited him well. He liked Hull because 'it is just a little wedge of England a bit off the beaten track . . . and the lonely place to me is always the exciting place.'[16] As he said in conversation, 'Librarianship suits me – I love the feel of libraries – and it has just the right blend of academic interest and administration that seems to match my particular talents, such as they are.'[17] He repeatedly said that he would not enjoy writing for a living even if he felt he could do it ('I write very, very slowly and with great pains'[18]) and an ambivalent attitude to work is the subject of several of his most well-known poems.

In the years when he had been trying to write novels, Larkin had also been writing poetry: 'I scribbled down poems which were nothing to me but they eventually began to form . . . the basis of *The Less Deceived*'.[19] Thirteen of these poems had already appeared in *XX Poems* which Larkin had privately printed in 1951 while he was in Northern Ireland. Larkin sent copies off to leading critics but it was mostly ignored, possibly because, as he admits, he had failed to put stamps of the right value on the envelopes but, more probably, because the predominant style of the poems was not yet then acceptable.[20] It was to become so with the work of the 'Movement' poets (see Chapter 3). Like many of these writers, Larkin published 'Pamphlet 21' in 1954 as part of the Fantasy Press series which contained poems to appear the following year in *The Less Deceived*. This volume became the foundation stone of Larkin's reputation and by 1973 had sold approximately ten thousand copies. It came about at the invitation of the publisher, George Hartley, who, having published some of Larkin's poems in the magazine *Listen*, was sure that it was warranted.

Larkin's third collection of poems did not appear until 1964 when *The Whitsun Weddings* was published by Faber (to whom Larkin had previously submitted and had rejected a collection in 1948 called *In the Grip of Light*). It sold well and 'a reprint was ordered shortly after publication'.[21] The following year Larkin was awarded the Queen's Gold Medal for Poetry, the first of many honours to be bestowed on him. A poet who wrote infrequently (at that time three or four completed poems a year), his next collection *High Windows*, appeared ten years later in 1974, although many of the poems had been printed in various publications over the intervening years. He had also been writing reviews of jazz records for *The Daily Telegraph* (later collected in book form as *All What Jazz*, Faber, 1970) between 1960 and 1968. As his publisher recalls, 'the book's reception by the critics ensured – for us it was a record for a volume of new verse – that we sold out a first printing of 6,000 in three weeks'.[22] That was to be the last collection issued, though a few poems did appear in journals and newspapers (see Bibliography).

*   *   *

Early in 1985 Larkin was admitted to hospital suffering from an illness of the throat. The nature of his illness was not disclosed, though his transferal in June to the intensive-care ward of the Hull Royal Infirmary was announced. On Monday 2 December, it was made known that he had died early that morning in the Nuffield Hospital, Hull. The illness had been cancer of the oesophagus, possibly related to the cigarettes he had been so fond of smoking.[23] It is said that he had refused to be told the nature of his illness. 'Larkin, the romantic recluse dies at 63,' was the headline in *The Guardian* while the *Morning Star* bleakly recorded 'Best-selling poet dies in private hospital'.

There followed many tributes in the press and on radio and television. *Newsnight* on BBC2 on 2 December contained quite a long item, incorporating extracts from the 'Monitor' programme made on his work in 1966 with John Betjeman, and an interview with his lifelong friend Kingsley Amis. The Radio 4 programme 'Kaleidoscope' the same night contained an interview with Christopher Ricks in whose view Larkin had 'really set high standards', had become 'an institution' who was 'moving' and 'memorable'. Other assessments quickly followed in print. Among the tributes to him that followed were readings each evening on BBC2 by contemporary poets and friends such as Andrew Motion and Gavin Ewart of their favourite Larkin poems. Later, in early 1986, there was an event at the Royal Festival Hall (18 February) devoted to Larkin and Robert Graves (who had also recently died) with readings and a reflection by John Wain. This was followed on 3 March by a commemorative programme 'Poetry of Departures' organised by the Poetry Society at the Riverside Studios, Hammersmith which included readings by Alan Bennett, Harold Pinter and Andrew Motion.

The nation's tribute came in the form of a 'Service In Memory of Philip Larkin, CH, CBE' on Friday 14 February at noon in Westminster Abbey which I had the fortune to attend. It was a bright, bitterly cold day with a biting north-east wind sweeping through central London, and the Abbey was crowded not just with figures from the worlds of literature and librarianship but also with people who simply had loved his work. (Charles Monteith, his publisher, was later to comment that the house of Faber had never had so many letters from 'ordinary' people on the death of one of their authors, expressing their gratitude.[24]) It might seem ironic that a poet who had written in so many poems of the finality of death and who had so openly declared his lack of religious belief should receive a service of thanksgiving in one of the nation's principal places of public worship, but the occasion was organised with tact and charity and did not seem sad. As the Bidding Prayer put it at the beginning of the service

> In particular on this day we commemorate with thanksgiving Philip Larkin who, possessing outstanding literary gifts, combined distinction with rare humility. We give thanks for his intellectual integrity which would not allow him to accept the consolations of a faith which he could not share and which would have delivered him from a fear of dying of which all his life he was haunted.

The Lesson (*Ecclesiasticus* 44, 1–15 'Let us now praise famous men . . .') was read by the Poet Laureate, Ted Hughes and then, after the Anthem and prayers, the Service concluded with Jill Balcon reading three of Larkin's poems and a jazz group playing pieces by Sidney Bechet and Bix Beiderbecke. One of the poems read was 'Church Going' which, as you will see when you come to read it, was a poignant, not to say wry, choice.

Larkin had ceased to write poetry some time before his death. In 1982 he told an interviewer that it was 'unlikely I shall write any more poems'[25] and, in what proved to be his last interview upon the award of the W. H. Smith Literary Award in 1984 for *Required Writing*, he was more explicit:

> Well, I haven't given poetry up, but I rather think poetry has given *me* up, which is a great sorrow to me, but not an enormous, crushing sorrow. It's a bit like going bald, you know, you can't do anything about it. I suppose the last substantial poem I wrote was about 1977, since which I haven't really been impelled to write anything, and I will stress the word 'impelled'. I think you don't write poems because you want to or try to but because you have to.[26]

In 'The South Bank Show' on him made by London Weekend Television in 1982 with Melvyn Bragg, Larkin had reflected on his earlier productiveness and reported that 'people tell me now I've got too comfortable'.[27] There may well have been some link in Larkin's case between discomfort and creativity, for, twenty years previously, anticipating what he was later to call his 'cycle-clip image',[28] he had told John Betjeman in conversation:

> I read that, you know, I'm a miserable sort of fellow writing of welfare state sub-poetry ... but I wonder if it ever occurs to the writer of criticism like that that really one *agrees* with them but what one writes is based so much on the kind of person one is and the kind of environment one's had and has now ...[29]

The BBC 'Monitor' programme from which this is taken was Larkin's only appearance on television. Nevertheless he did give a number of interviews, which is perhaps slightly surprising for a man who believed that it was 'very sensible not to let people know what you're like'.[30] Although essentially a private man, his success inevitably made him into a public figure:

> Honorary Doctor of Literature of the Universities of Belfast (1960), Warwick (1973), Sussex (1974), New University of Ulster (1983)
> Queens Award for Poetry (1974)
> A. C. Benson Silver Medal, Royal Society of Literature (1975)
> C.B.E. (1975)
> Fellow of the Royal Society of Literature
> Coventry Award of Merit (1978)
> Companion of Literature (1978)
> Personal Chair at the University of Hull
> W. H. Smith Literary Award (1984)
> Companion of Honour (1985)

He was also active on behalf of his fellow writers, as Anthony Thwaite noted in an addendum to *The Times* obituary:

> he served on the Literary Panel of the Arts Council of Great Britain, was particularly active in first setting up and then guiding the Arts Council's National Manuscript Collection of Contemporary Writers in conjunction with the British Museum, was Chairman for several years of the Poetry Book Society, was Chairman of the judges for the Booker Prize in 1977, and as a widely respected librarian was a prominent member of the Standing Conference of National and University Libraries.[31]

The awards and honours bestowed on Larkin are testimony not to the value of his poetry alone but to that of his writings as a whole: in addition to his four volumes of verse and two novels, there is also *The Oxford Book of Twentieth-Century Verse* (1973) which he edited, the collection of jazz criticism *All What Jazz* (1970) which he wrote while critic for *The Daily Telegraph*, and most recently, *Required Writing: Miscellaneous Pieces 1955–82* (1983) which won him the W. H. Smith Literary Award.

Required Writing was also an immediate popular success which Larkin, modestly, put down partly to the acumen of his publisher in issuing the book at a reasonable price just before Christmas. Yet in talking about the book, Larkin described how seriously he took writing critical essays and how difficult he found it:

> I really did put my effort into the reviews. When I review I really take it very seriously. I really do read the whole book more than once and I write pages of notes and that kind of thing. It takes me an awfully long time and that is what I'd really like to be judged by.[32]

Interestingly, Larkin also saw the book as a form of 'writer's biography':

> I like to think it *is* a readable book, and an amusing book and an interesting book for people who like literature ... I suppose, and rather reluctantly I suppose, it is a kind of concealed autobiography.[33].

Larkin's 'reluctance' is understandable, for privacy clearly mattered to him and losing it in order to write as he feels he had to was a high price to pay. Writing about Larkin himself rather than his work is somewhat daunting for, as a friend of his has pointed out, 'imperfect conclusions about Philip's personality are rife in literary criticism'.[34] Nevertheless, it is possible to give some idea of his temperament and opinions from remarks he has made to interviewers. Solitude was important to him – 'I see life more as an affair of solitutde diversified by company than an affair of company diversified by solitude ... I'm very fond of people, but it's difficult to get people without company'.[35] So, remaining unmarried was a natural consequence of this need. Politically, he had 'always been right-wing' for, 'while not being a political thinker I suppose I identify the Right with certain virtues and the Left with certain vices' (the former being 'thrift, hard work, reverence, desire to preserve', the latter 'idleness, greed and treason').[36] His general outlook has been described as pessimistic, and fairly so, for he admitted to thinking it 'very much easier to imagine happiness than to experience it' and admitted a dread of 'endless extinction'.[37] On the other hand, Kingsley Amis, who knew him for many years, described him as the 'most enlivening companion I have ever known' and saw Larkin as treating 'the world with jovial acerbity'.[38] And indeed dry humour is a frequent counterpoint in Larkin's poems to the bleaker statements.

Biography – help or hindrance?

In speaking of Larkin, Amis has also remarked on 'the total honesty that marks both him and his work'.[40] Should the reader then

assume that the life and the art are inextricably linked? Larkin
himself said to George Hartley before the publication of *The Less
Deceived* that 'my poems are nothing if not personal'[40] and
Andrew Motion considers that 'to a large extent . . . the poems *are*
autobiographical'.[41] Should we deduce from such remarks that the
narrator in each poem is to be identified with Larkin himself? What
do you gain if you do assume this? Or, conversely, can such
biographical knowledge actually hinder appreciation of the poems?

The relationship between biography and interpretation,
criticism and evaluation has given rise to a great deal of discussion
especially in our century. And this is likely to continue, for the
relevant arguments each way always seem more or less convincing
according to the writer whose work is selected for evidence.
Sometimes knowledge of the life is a help in exegesis – that is,
assists in explaining obscurities and ironing out difficulties. Yet
such knowledge might encourage the reader to forget that the poem
is the work of an artist, that it is consciously wrought for a purpose
and not 'life transcribed in ink'. Then again, it cannot be denied
that a page was written by a particular hand, so there has to be
some connection circumstantially between the hand and the words
and so to the mind that directs the hand. And what of the opinion
the reader forms of the work? Is that influenced by what is known
about the author ('He seems malicious, therefore he is a bad artist
. . .')? And should one work be read in the context of others by the
same writer? Some biographical knowledge, even of the skimpiest
kind, is needed to do that. These are all questions to think about
while reading the poems discussed in the following chapters. There
are not necessarily any hard and fast answers to them but, by
Chapter 7, they should be more clearly focused by your reading of
Larkin's work.

2. What Kind of Poet is Larkin?

Larkin, like the late Sir John Betjeman (1906–84) (whose work he greatly admired), is by contemporary standards an immensely popular poet, as the sales of his volumes show. He said on several occasions that he found pleasure not in being written about by academics but in receiving letters from members of the reading public who recognise their own experiences in his poems. Therein lies one of the reasons for his popularity: his poems usually start from a recognisable, circumstantial situation and this makes them immediately accessible. Take, for example, 'Mr Bleaney' in *The Whitsun Weddings* (p. 10) where, in seven four-line stanzas, a whole drama is unfolded involving Mr Bleaney, the speaker, the landlady, and, finally, (by implication) humanity itself. Nothing in the poem presents any real difficulty to the understanding. Perhaps the reference to 'the Bodies' will not instantly be understood by readers unfamiliar with the manufacture of carbodies in the British Midlands, and the four 'aways', i.e. 'away football matches', need to be explained too those who do not do football pools. Yet these are characteristically precise details which set the poem firmly in a local context. Larkin is particularly skilful at evoking a situation by such chosen detail: so here, the curtains 'thin and frayed' and of the wrong length, 'the saucer-souvenir' and the low-wattage light bulb capture the dinginess of the rented room. The 'drama', as I have termed it, is revealed through a verbal structure, apparently simple and artless but in fact unobtrusively skilled.

The first three stanzas use: reported speech by the landlady; recollected observation through the eyes of the speaker; his reply; then a move into present time:

... So it happens that I lie
where Mr Bleaney lay, ...

The pivot of the poem is the fact that Mr Bleaney and the speaker are both in the same 'hired box', which prompts the sombre fear

> That how we live measures our own nature,
> and at his age having no more to show
> Than one hired box should make him pretty sure
> He warranted no better . . .

The move from a particular, documented case to a wider, general perspective in which 'we' are moved to consider how our own lives might be evaluated is characteristic of many of Larkin's poems; while the integration of recollected past, observed present and linking meditation is achieved so subtly that one hardly notices any 'change of gear', though this is in fact what has occurred.

Also characteristic of much of Larkin's work is his insight into the lives of individuals, especially as in this case where they are sensed to be, if not inadequate, at least trapped within an unsatisfactory and unsatisfying situation. The lives of Mr Bleaney and his former landlady are sketched in inks of irony and dark humour: the garden which he took 'in hand' is in fact 'tussocky, littered', and her dependence on his utterly predictable routine is what he has to tell himself is 'home'. The overall mood of the poem is chilling and Larkin's choice of words contributes greatly to this impression. The name 'Mr Bleaney' suggests 'bleakness', 'lean' and 'meaney'; then there is 'Frinton', 'frigid', and 'fusty', all of which combine to suggest a cold dreariness.

Another reason for the accessibility of the poem is that it is cast in a traditional form – seven quatrains of iambic pentameters with a regular rhyme of 'abab'. Not all Larkin's work is written in what is a conventional English mode but, on the whole, he uses established forms and chooses them to suit what he has to say, for as he remarked in an interview, 'at any level that matters, form and content are indivisible'.[1]

The quality of insight evident in 'Mr Bleaney' is also to be seen when Larkin writes about animals. His best known poem of this kind is 'At Grass', (*The Less Deceived*, p. 45) and in this as in several others the animals are seen to be victims of the human world. The retired race horses in 'At Grass', now freed, 'gallop for what must be joy', the implication being that formerly they were spurred to do so. In a richly ambiguous two lines, the speaker asks:

> Do memories plague their ears like flies?
> They shake their heads. . . .

The suggestion that they might be answering the unspoken question establishes with quiet humour a bond of understanding between the speaker and the horses. 'Myxomatosis' (*The Less Deceived*, p. 31), about a rabbit found dying of the disease, has the speaker in the last two lines thinking compassionately

> You may have thought things would come right again
> If you could only keep quite still and wait.

The compassion in this poem is tinged with anger, a combination which appears with great force when Larkin is writing in a later poem ('The Old Fools', *High Windows* p. 19) about people who, likewise, are in some sense victims.

Many of Larkin's poems have an urban setting. In *The Whitsun Weddings* two poems take their origin in commercial advertisements, as in 'Essential Beauty' (p. 42) which humorously describes one as being pasted

> In frames as large as rooms that face all ways
> And block the ends of streets with giant loaves

Larkin writes about places and situations which are familiar to most people; none of his poems has a foreign setting or relies on knowledge of myth. He writes of English towns, high-street stores and sights familiar to all, as in these lines from 'Ambulances' (*The Whitsun Weddings*, p. 33):

> Then children strewn on steps or road,
> Or women coming from the shops
> Past smells of different dinners, see
> A wild white face that overtops
> Red stretcher-blankets momently
> As it is carried in and stowed.

One of his subjects is the place of a regular job in shaping people's lives and the best known of these poems, 'Toads' (*The Less Deceived*, p. 32) and 'Toads Revisited' (*The Whitsun Weddings*, p. 18), are amusing and serious reflections on the way people spend their time, whether avoiding the 'toad work' or having it 'squat on' their lives, a theme taken up in more sober fashion in the trilogy 'Livings' (*High Windows*, p. 13).

The passage of time is another recurrent subject in Larkin's work and, indeed, he has said that one of his reasons for writing is to rescue experiences from time:

> I write about experiences, often quite simple, everyday experiences
> which somehow acquire some sort of special meaning for me, and I
> write poems about them to preserve them. You see, I want to express
> the experience in a poem so that it remains preserved, unchanging;
> and I then hope that other people will come upon this experience,
> pickled as it were in verse, and it will mean something to them,

sound some chord in their own recollection, perhaps, or show them something familiar in a new light.[2]

Human beings exist in time: they are born and they experience death, and this is Larkin's major theme. He has admitted to dreading 'endless extinction' and written very powerfully on the notion in an uncollected poem 'Aubade'.[3] 'Next, Please' in *'The Less Deceived'* (p. 20) employs and develops the metaphor of a 'sparkling armada of promises' only to conclude that in reality

> Only one ship is seeking us, a black
> Sailed unfamiliar, towing at her back
> A huge and birdless silence.

In 'Nothing to be Said' (*The Whitsun Weddings*, p. 11) the reader is told that 'Life is slow dying' and in two longer poems in *High Windows* ('The Old Fools', p. 19, and 'The Building', p. 24) the subject is treated with great imaginative power and a striking charge of emotion. 'The Building', never actually named as the hospital it is, begins descriptively but an ominous, threatening note soon sounds:

> Higher than the handsomest hotel
> The lucent comb shows up for miles, but see,
> All round it close-ribbed streets rise and fall
> Like a great sigh out of the last century.
> The porters are scruffy; what keep drawing up
> At the entrance are not taxis; and in the hall
> As well as creepers hangs a frightening smell.

Not naming the arriving vehicles as ambulances adds to the sense of fear and the unknown. They are bringing people to the 'Building' to 'confess that something has gone wrong' and the parallel between this building and churches is developed in the course of the poem. By the final stanza, the conclusion is reached that

> ... unless its powers
> Outbuild cathedrals nothing contravenes
> The coming dark, though crowds each evening try,
> With wasteful, weak, propitiatory flowers.

It is his propensity for writing about death, failures and disappointments that has earned Larkin the reputation of being a purveyor of sadness and pessimism, the frequent evidence of humour and the ever-present wit notwithstanding. Whether or not this amounts to a 'philosophy' is a question to bear in mind when reading the poems we will look at in detail in subsequent chapters. Nevertheless, it would be misleading to suggest that all Larkin's work is redolent of sadness and death, and even in 'The Building' there is a lyrical passage expressing an emphatic desire for life. He has also written poems like 'Show Saturday' and 'To the Sea' (*High Windows*, p. 37, p. 9) which record in carefully observed detail people together at leisure, as in these lines from the first of those two poems:

> Folks sit about on bales
> Like great straw dice. For each scene is linked by spaces
> Not given to anything much, where kids scrap, freed,
> While their owners stare different ways with incurious faces.

In poems of this kind, there is an underlying, almost unspoken sense of celebration, as in these concluding lines from 'Show Saturday':

> . . . something they share
> That breaks ancestrally each year into
> Regenerate union. Let it always be there.

In these two poems, the speaker is the observer, never the participant. In 'To the Sea', he recalls how as a child 'happy at being on my own,/. I searched the sand for Famous Cricketers' and then, how as an adult, 'Strange to it now, I watch the cloudless scene'. Being outside events, and thus solitary – this provides a recurrent theme in Larkin's work, though often as a positive state and not at all to be regretted. (See for example, 'Here', *The Whitsun Weddings*, p. 9 and 'Vers de Société, *High Windows*, p. 35) One of the reasons Larkin liked living in Hull is that 'it is so far away from everywhere else'[4] and this attraction to lonely places led to his being photographed for one interview in a graveyard.

I began this chapter by stressing that Larkin's poetry is readily accessible to the general reader and we shall look at the reason for this in a moment. None the less, sometimes the meaning does take considerable working out. Thus, 'Mr Bleaney', straightforward enough in one respect, includes an eight-line two-stanza sentence whose syntactical complexity ends the poem on a strongly enigmatic note. Or there is 'Sympathy in White Major' (*High Windows*, p. 11) which appears to be about a man mixing himself a gin and tonic and indulging in self-ironic toasting to his art. Indeed, it *is* about this but its particular title and the stress on whiteness[5] remain enigmatic unless you are familiar with the nineteenth-century French poet Théophile Gautier's '*Symphonie en Blanc Majeur*'. If you are, it is then clear that Larkin is deliberately setting his self-mockery against the harmonious concord of Gautier's world of '*implacable blancheur*'. Similarly, 'Dry-Point' (*The Less Deceived*, p. 19) takes a little working out (and some knowledge of art techniques to realise that the title is a pun) before it becomes clear that it is a poem about post-coital disillusion. These two poems are more difficult than most of Larkin's because of the deliberately oblique approach to his subject; in recent years, critical commentary on Larkin has tended to stress this 'symbolist' element in his work, and I shall have more to say about this in a later chapter.

Other poems not of this kind begin with a situation or incident which is recounted in a straightforward fashion but which leads to a concluding statement of almost 'metaphysical' wit. 'No Road' (*The Less Deceived*, p. 26) begins by describing the end of a relationship by means of the metaphor of a road between two properties left unused, and concludes with the speaker imagining a world where the road no longer even exists i.e. where the past could be wiped out. His final statement is that

> Not to prevent it is my will's fulfilment.
> Willing it, my ailment.

Conclusions of this kind, simultaneously presenting two possible points of view, are common in Larkin's work.

The balance I have been describing between the accessible and the more sophisticated sides of Larkin's work is reflected in the use he makes of two poetic 'voices', one demotic and the other more eloquent, played off against each other. 'Mr Bleaney', where the landlady's remarks in uneducated everyday English contrast with the measured sweep of the concluding eight lines, is a good example of this contrast. Larkin's use of the occasional unfamiliar but always exact word is an aspect of his more poetic voice, and 'Toads' (*The Less Deceived*, p. 32) contains more of these than usual. In listing those who live on 'their wits', the speaker instances 'losels, loblolly-men' and most readers would have to go to a dictionary to discover the latter was first used in 1604 to mean a 'rustic bumpkin'. Similarly, later in the poem, 'hunkers', apart from its alliterative value in the line ('hunkers' – 'heavy' – 'hard'), is very precise following on from 'squats', as it denotes the action of resting on bent ankles. Such a deliberate use of vocabulary is all the more effective for the sparing use Larkin makes of it.

Larkin deliberately cultivates the approachable manner of his writing, reflecting his view that art should give pleasure and need not be 'difficult'. This is something he learned from Hardy (see p. 29) and it is evidently one of the principles behind the selection he made for *The Oxford Book of Twentieth-Century Verse* which he is pleased to describe as a 'readable book'. 'I made twentieth-century poetry sound nice.'[6] Concomitant with this idea is his objection to 'modernism' which he once described as denoting a 'quality of irresponsibility peculiar to this century, because, in his view, artists working in that mode made comprehensibility and pleasure the least of their aims. T. S. Eliot's dictum that poetry in the twentieth century was likely 'to be difficult' was inimical to Larkin, and the number of letters from ordinary readers received by his publisher on his death shows how successfully he avoided this himself.

3. Novelist into Poet

Larkin was by no means exceptional in starting his writing career with fiction: G. B. Shaw wrote six novels before his first play, and George Orwell was a novelist before he turned to journalism. In retrospect, Larkin himself is inclined to the view that, in reality, he was always a poet despite his ambition 'to be a novelist'. In an interview with Ian Hamilton, he reflected on *Jill* and *A Girl in Winter*:

> Looking back on them, I think they were over-sized poems. They were certainly written with intense care for detail. If one word was used on page 15, I didn't re-use it on page 115. But they're not very good novels.[1]

Contrary to the author's opinion, many readers have thought that both novels are impressive achievements and they remain in print today forty years after first publication. They were both written at a time when Larkin was finding his way as a writer, working in both poetry and prose, and, though differing stylistically, they share similar themes which were to recur in the later verse. The first novel *Jill*, was begun when Larkin was twenty-one and had just left Oxford. As a prefatory note states, the main location of the story 'in time and place – the Michaelmas Term at Oxford University in 1940 – is more or less real' though 'the characters are imaginary'.

Briefly, the story is about a shy, working-class boy from 'Huddlesford', John Kemp, who having won a scholarship to Oxford, finds himself in a confusing world alien to his experience. His predicament is exacerbated by the fact that he shares rooms with Geoffrey Warner, a selfish extrovert from a minor public school. There are others from his own background in the college (typified by the hard-working Northern scholar Whitbread), but Warner's way of life and circle of friends, whose company Kemp cannot to some extent avoid sharing, at first appal and then begin to fascinate him. He is made use of by Warner who borrows his belongings and then laughs at him behind his back. Overhearing an episode of this kind further diminishes Kemp's self-esteem so that 'once they had shown him that he was despicable, he instantly saw himself as fifty times more despicable than they thought him' (pp. 111–12). His feelings of self-disgust are intensified by the fact that, consciously and unconsciously, he has been adopting Warner's mannerisms and doing him favours in an attempt to win his friendship.

Overhearing Warner's real opinion of him precipitates a crisis which prompts Kemp, in his isolation, to fabricate a life for himself in which he has an imaginary sister, Jill. This is his only defence against Warner's outrageous treatment of him (e.g. demanding that Kemp write his essays): 'he had no means of retaliation – only Jill'.[3] He goes to the extent of devising letters from her which he leaves lying around in the hope that Warner will read them (which he doesn't). In a letter to 'Jill', Kemp recounts the humiliating events of his first month at Oxford, but recasts them in a more favourable light by 'describing, relating, falsifying' (p. 133).[4] This fantasy world in which 'Jill' embodies for him beauty and innocence sustains him for a while but cannot last and this makes his situation worse than ever:

> It was impossible to make friends with Christopher and Elizabeth [his girl-friend], and that was the only thing he wanted to do, now that he had awoken hopelessly from his attempt to build a world around Jill. He knew that one more world had crumbled to bits under his hand. (p. 155)

The story then takes a turn towards the final crisis when Kemp sees a girl who exactly resembles the 'Jill' of his fantasy. He becomes obsessed with finding out who she is and, coincidentally, it turns out she is a cousin of Warner's girl-friend Elizabeth. His attempt to invite her to tea is thwarted by Elizabeth. In addition to his isolation, Kemp is troubled by his sexuality which is awoken by Warner's girl-friend. Yet, when Warner boasts of a planned seduction, Kemp, thinking of himself, 'knew with a sickened certainty that he could never sustain that position; that he would, in fact, turn and run long before it came' (p. 170). Finally, after an episode where Kemp returns to his bombed home town, the crisis occurs. Discovering the whereabouts of a party where Jill is to be present, Kemp gets very drunk and, seeing her approaching, kisses her, whereupon he is set on by Warner and thrown into a fountain. The novel ends with Kemp in a sick-bed suffering from pneumonia, experiencing strange dreams about the stolen kiss and reflecting on

> . . . the fact that in life he had been cheated of her was not the whole truth. Somewhere, in dreams, perhaps, on some other level, they had interlocked and he had had his own way as completely as in life he had been denied it. And this dream showed that love died, whether fulfilled or unfulfilled. He grew confused whether she had accepted him or not, since the result was the same: and as this confusion increased, it spread to fulfillment or unfulfillment, which merged and became inseparable. The difference between them vanished. (p. 242)

As this resumé indicates. *Jill* shows an impressive psychological insight into the consequences of isolation, and how this can be related to confusion of identity. Kemp is shown trying to adopt other people's personalities:

> For the lecture he decided to be Mr Crouch [his former school teacher], nodding his head wisely at intervals and making a few microscopic jottings, to be copied and expanded later; by eleven, he remembered, the public houses would be open, and he could be Christopher and stand drinking in a bar. (p. 96)

Kemp's attitude towards Christopher (one of Warner's 'set') is ambiguous, for he admires and tries to emulate his insouciance and yet is constantly humiliated by him and his friends. In turn, he uses his 'friendship' with Warner as a way of trying to impress the set of working-class, hard-working scholars, the embodiment of whom, Whitbread, he eventually betrays by condoning the stealing of his cake and dismissing him with the comment:

> 'Oh, he's an awful man. . . . have all you want.' (p. 175)

Food imagery, as Andrew Motion has pointed out, plays an important and complex part in the novel.[2] The first chapter shows Kemp unhappily uncertain as to whether it is socially acceptable to eat his sandwich lunch in a full train compartment on his way to Oxford.

> . . . at one o'clock he had grown desperate and he slunk along to the lavatory, where he locked himself in and bolted a few of his sandwiches before a furious rattling at the door made him cram the

rest out of the ventilator, noisily flush the unused water-closet and go
back to his seat. His return might have been a prearranged signal: the
shorter and fatter of the two old ladies said: 'Well!' in a pleased way,
and produced a leather shopping-bag from which she took napkins,
packets of sandwiches. . . . :p. 22)

Kemp is then offered food by all present:

In the end he was forced to accept not only three sandwiches from
the ladies, but a piece of cake from the girl and a quarter of the
clergyman's apple. He kept his eyes fixed on the dirty floor as he
chewed, utterly humiliated. (p. 23)

This is the first of many humiliations where Kemp's doubts about
himself and inadequacies are conveyed through episodes in which
detail about food is prominent. Warner steals his butter, causing
Elizabeth to remark (overheard by Kemp)

'Well, of all the – – –! It's too bad. He *must* be a feeble sort of worm.'
(p. 111)

Later in the novel, at breakfast one day, Whitbread displays
dexterity in eating kippers while

John removed a handful of bones from his mouth. (p. 159)

Tea-parties are a feature of the Oxford life described in the novel,
and Kemp's attempt to hold one for himself and 'Jill' is his final
failure. He goes to great lengths to provide attractive fare:

He bought here and there a number of fruit tarts, a jam roll and a
sponge cake filled with jam, and a fruit cake. He carried them most
carefully and watched the clean new bags for any strain that would
show that the jam was crawling out. (p. 196)

John, because of experience at home, could choose lettuces with
sound fresh hearts, and radishes that were not fibrous; the
newspaper parcel he carried away was light and damp. (p. 197)

But Gillian ('Jill') is prevented from attending, a disappointment made
humilitatingly public by the arrival of Warner's cronies who, beginning to eat the food prepared for her, reduce Kemp to making a

queer noise . . . it ended as a semi-articulated cry, shaken with a
curious blubbering vibrato. (p. 202)

He is forced to recognise that

All his life he had imagined people were hostile to him and wanted to
hurt him; now he knew he had been right and all the worst fears of
childhood were realised. (p. 203)

Good food and its elegant consumption come to stand for–the

things that have eluded Kemp, and always will. Instead, he is stuck with Whitbread who offers coffee essence and yesterday's buns and eats 'a whole potato' (p. 99) at a time.

Among the things that elude Kemp is any kind of contentment with his sexuality. Stirred by Warner's intentions on his girl-friend, Kemp finds that:

> Quite to his surprise an agitation was beginning to fume up inside him as if he were being threatened in some way. (p. 169)

Prominent in the dreams he has in his sickness after the final crisis is the memory of the kiss he stole from 'Jill'. Larkin handles this aspect of his personality with tact and integrates it with other aspects of the character he portrays.

That the title of this first novel is *Jill*, not *John Kemp* or *Scholarship Boy* or whatever, is significant in determining the meaning of the novel. Kemp's solution to his predicament (writing letters to a non-existent person who then becomes the subject of a short fiction within the novel) might appear to strain the reader's credulity. Is Kemp simply insane? He is undoubtedly unbalanced, though behaving reasonably according to his own confused lights, but the fantasy world that he creates, 'Jill', is perhaps better understood in another way. It is, in its own peculiar fashion, the act of an artist, for Kemp creates and modifies a world, and one which is outside his own experience. In a different way, this is what Larkin is doing too. Perhaps, then, *Jill* is in part a model about the writing of fiction and the function of art. Kemp's 'art' provides him with solace and, in the absence of happiness, a form of consolation – a theme which recurs later in the poetry (see 'Reasons for Attendance' in *The Less Deceived*, p. 18). The eventual collapse of this defence and the subsequent disillusion brings Kemp to a greater awareness of his situation as he reflects on his sick-bed, and this is another theme of the poetry (see, for example, 'Sunny Prestatyn', *The Whitsun Weddings*, p. 35, discussed below, p. 57).

Larkin described his two novels as being written with 'an intense care for detail', and *Jill* is indeed rich in conscious artistry. The structure of the novel is one instance of this, moving from narrative to fiction within fiction, to dramatised 'flashback' (Kemp's school days), and back to reported narrative. Another example is the deliberate symmetry of the two moments when eggs are broken (food, again). The first occurs when Kemp recalls his attempt at home to boil an egg:

> he had placed the egg on the kitchen table, looking round for a saucepan, and, before he could stop it, the egg rolled over the edge and smashed on the brick floor. (p. 42)

The second occurs in the 'flashback' episode when Kemp's teacher, Mr Crouch, has finished his tea and is contemplating finding a suitable pupil to groom for a scholarship:

> Picking up the empty eggshell that his spoon had scoured clean, he gazed at it solemnly. What should he do? Should he indulge this fancy? He sat grinning, increasing the pressure of his thumb and forefinger, until with a sudden smash the shell collapsed. (p. 68)

The 'egg' in both cases, of course, is to be Kemp himself. By enabling him to move into an alien world, Crouch is ultimately responsible for the crisis which occurs in his pupil's life. There are other deliberate touches, like the description of Kemp when he has added to his wardrobe by buying a new tie:

> As soon as he got outside, he went down a public lavatory to put it on. He was so nervous when he emerged that for all practical purposes he was a walking bow-tie. (p. 98)

Or, there is the manner in which the character Whitbread is built up: Larkin clearly had a lot of fun with this, and sometimes comes close to caricature. (Why does Whitbread but not Kemp have a 'Northern' accent?) Nevertheless, some of the effects are amusing and Whitbread's carefulness and stolidity are cleverly captured by small details:

> Whitbread seemed to take a fancy to John, and after the meal was over asked him back to his room for coffee. They crossed the pitch-dark quadrangle together, Whitbread holding a bicycle flashlamp to show the way, and climbed to a tiny set of rooms in the attics, where a dull fire smouldered. (p. 51)

There is a poignancy about the final scenes of the novel where Kemp lies in his sick-bed about to be visited by his parents who are being shown the way by an oblivious Warner, breezily leaving the college at the end of term with his girl-friend. The strongest feeling lingering through these final pages is a kind of hopelessness and the sense that probably nothing very much matters as it is beyond individual control:

> Then if there was no difference between love fulfilled and love unfulfilled, how could there be any difference between any other pair of opposites? Was he not freed, for the rest of his life, from choice?
>   For what could it matter? Let him take this course, or this course, but still behind the mind, on some other level, the way he had rejected was being simultaneously worked out and the same conclusion being reached. What did it matter which road he took if they both led to the same place? (p. 243)

The theme is repeated, with some variation, in the second

novel and re-emerges again in Larkin's poetry. In this way, these two novels have much interest for those concerned to chart Larkin's 'development' (a term he loathed), apart from their intrinsic value. Like many first novels, *Jill* is clearly in some sense autobiographical and, for all its oddities, it is well written and its enduring readability is easily understood.

There are clearly autobiographical elements in the second novel, *A Girl in Winter*. The protagonist, Katherine Lind, works in a public library in wartime (as did Larkin) during a bitterly cold winter (as was the winter of 1947 when the novel appeared). Like *Jill*, it is a carefully structured novel, in three parts, the first and the third set within one day and the middle part a 'flashback' to an earlier period.

In the first part, Katherine Lind (a lonely refugee) decides to make contact with the Fennels, an English family with whom, as an adolescent, she had spent one summer. This first part of the novel is largely taken up describing her drab life and unlikeable colleagues, in particular her superior, Mr Anstey, whom she regards with thinly veiled contempt. This section concludes when Katherine receives a letter promising an immediate visit from Robin Fennel, the son of the family, and she is filled with misgivings for reasons she cannot quite identify.

The middle retrospective section recounts her adolescent visit to the Fennels at (she supposed) the invitation of Robin who is her pen-friend. The visit is in many ways painful for the young Katherine who feels confused by the correct, middle-class Fennel family and especially by the self-assured and meticulously, correctly pleasant Robin. Eventually she discovers that 'at some untraceable point she had fallen in love with him' (p. 127) and, bewildered, she cannot work out why, having taken the trouble to invite her, he yet remains distant. It is Robin's sister, Jane, a down-to-earth woman of twenty-five, who reveals that the invitation had not been Robin's idea at all but hers, simply to alleviate her own boredom. Disillusioned, Katherine is disappointed about her visit:

> She had come expecting to solve a mystery, and had found at the end there was no mystery to solve. From what she had been told, she had been invited partly out of politeness and partly to divert Jane's alleged boredom. (p. 165)

Jane and Robin are contrasting figures: he, as his sister puts it, is 'ordinary, down to the last button' (p. 107), and has his life carefully planned out for the foreseeable future. The older and more realistic Jane is shown in the final pages of this section making a compromise between her real feelings and practical alternatives

by accepting an offer of marriage from a family friend whose
relentlessly extrovert and unimaginative manner is well summed up
in his surname, Stormalong.

The third part of the novel returns us to the present with
Katherine now expecting Robin's visit. First we are given an
account of her taking stock of her life. As a refugee in England, she
has contacted the Fennels out of loneliness. She realises that

> . . . she had not been facing the facts. To live from day to day, as she
> had been doing, shut out the past, but it shut out the future too . . .
> (p. 182)

The winter of the title is not simply literal: it is a metaphor for her
world which is 'like a painting of a winter landscape in neutral
colours' (p. 126). There is then a short episode in which Katherine
returns a handbag to its rightful owner, a Miss Parbury, a
somewhat pitiful spinster about to sacrifice her own chance of
marriage to the unpleasant Mr Anstey in order to look after her
ailing mother. In a row with Anstey shortly afterwards, Katherine is
able to use this information to exact revenge for his rudeness. In the
meantime, Robin has left a message cancelling his visit. At home,
Katherine, reflecting on the events of the day, realises that there will
be other 'Miss Greens, Miss Parburys, Mr Ansteys' but resolves
that, for her, there 'would be no more Robins' (p. 216). She
consciously adopts a stoical outlook:

> Life would be happy insofar as she was happy, sad insofar as she was
> sad. The happiness would depend on her youth and health, and
> would help no-one. (p. 215)

Ironically, Katherine has no sooner made this resolve than Robin
turns up at her door unexpectedly. Although both recognise, in the
course of conversation, that they were never really friends, she
allows him to stay with her for the night as 'an unimportant
kindness' (p. 243). The novel ends with a lyrical passage about their
dreams:

> Unsatisfied dreams rose and fell about them, crying out against their
> implacability, but in the end glad that such order, such destiny
> existed. Against this knowledge, the heart, the will, and all that made
> for protest, could at least sleep. (p. 248)

Like John Kemp in *Jill*, Katherine is an isolated figure who has a
crisis which brings a new understanding of her position. Both
novels end with their principal characters in dreams which are
'unsatisfied' and in which 'unfulfillment' figures. The language of
the final paragraph with its emphasis on feeling and the 'heart' and,
indeed, the mood of the novel as a whole is strikingly similar to

many of the poems in *The North Ship*, Larkin's first collection
published in 1945. For example:

> If grief could burn out
> Like a sunken coal,
> The heart would rest quiet

> (XVIII; p. 30)

The collection contains one poem which distinctly prefigures the
novel and begins:

> I see a girl dragged by the wrists
> Across a dazzling field of snow,
> And there is nothing in me that resists.

> (XX; p. 32)

The passivity of that final line is characteristic – a stoical
acceptance of existence in which chance and lack of choice seem to
rule. This is what Katherine Lind finally arrives at – an attitude or
outlook which figures frequently in the later poetry ('No Road',
The Less Deceived, p. 26 is a good example – see Chaper 2). This
bleak vision is well expressed in a series of metaphors recounting
her thoughts towards the end of the novel:

> . . . life ceased to be a confused stumbling from one illumination to
> another, a series of unconnected clearings in a tropical forest, and
> became a flat landscape, wry and rather small, with a few
> unforgettable landmarks somewhat resembling a stretch of fenland,
> where an occasional dyke or broken fence shows up for miles, and
> the sails of a mill turn all day long in the steady wind. (p. 183)

Jane Fennel's boredom – 'there isn't anything I want to do' (p. 152)
– is another expression of this meaninglessness which figures baldly
in 'Dockery and Son' (*The Whitsun Weddings*, p. 38):

> Life is first boredom, then fear.

The paragraph quoted above illustrates well one of the several
styles of writing Larkin employs in *A Girl in Winter*, a consciously
'poetic' prose with careful attention to language which makes the
novel more akin to a poem than *Jill*. The first chapter, which is in
the nature of a prose poem setting the winter scene as a preface to
the narrative, shows this 'lyrical' style. It begins:

> There had been no more snow during the night, but because the frost
> continued so that the drifts lay where they had fallen, people told
> each other there was more to come. And when it grew lighter, it
> seemed that they were right, for there was no sun, only one vast shell
> of cloud over the fields and woods. In contrast to the snow the sky

looked brown. Indeed, without the snow the morning would have
resembled a January nightfall, for what light there was seemed to rise
up from it. (p. 11)

Alongside this kind of writing is a more quotidian 'prose' style in
which the action of the novel is cast. Andrew Motion has likened
these two 'languages' to 'Yeatsian and Hardyesque dictions'[3] and
the comparison is apt for it was at this time that Larkin was moving
as an apprentice poet from one master to the other. The
'Hardyesque' aspect of the novel is evident in the careful
employment of circumstantial detail to create a fictional world, and
the memorable descriptions of very ordinary events and actions.
This, again, is a quality of Larkin's later verse. (For example, the
gymkhana in *A Girl in Winter*, p. 110 looks forward to Larkin's
later poem 'Show Saturday' – *High Windows*, p. 37.)

Like *Jill*, Larkin's second novel has its own intrinsic interest
and continues to attract readers. Nevertheless, it is something of an
oddity and is not without weaknesses. For one thing, the
characterisation is sometimes thin: Mr and Mrs Fennel are never
more than cardboard figures, and Jack Stormalong whom the
author evidently despises, is frankly hardly credible. The main
character, Katherine, is puzzling: we are given her thoughts in great
detail (indeed, we see most of the action through them) and yet she
remains shadowy. We know that she is 'foreign' and this quality is
constantly stressed but we are not told where she comes from. No
doubt this is quite deliberate and intended to 'free' her from any
associations, to underscore the existentialist nature of her
experience of life and amplify her isolation but, like the fantasy
episode in *Jill*, it strikes an odd note. Both novels are interesting
additions to the library of fiction though decidedly strange ones in
some ways.

In the first chapter, I touched on possible reasons for Larkin
abandoning the novel genre and it is a question which has intrigued
many of his readers who have found pleasure in the two that were
published. The novelist Barbara Pym, whom he admired and helped
get republished and who became a friend in later life, speculated
aloud in a letter to him:

> I was amazed at *Jill*. Such maturity – and detachment and,
> 'Sentiments to which every bosom returns an echo . . .' it was
> difficult to believe it had been written by a boy of 21! Of course it is
> *very* well written and observed too – I don't mean to sound surprised
> at that, but I hadn't expected it to be *quite* so good. And
> remembering *A Girl in Winter* one wonders why you didn't go on
> writing fiction, and regrets it. I suppose you were *too good* and
> didn't perhaps sell enough, and then you preferred writing poetry?

But couldn't you possibly give us a novel now and again – those nine years in a northern university ... surely, you are being rather *selfish*?[4]

Larkin's mature view of the two genres is expressed in the address he made in 1977 as chairman of the judges in the Booker–McConell prize competition for new novels. Rather surprisingly, he told the audience that

I consider the novel at its best to be the maturest of our literary forms

because

In a novel, the emotion has to be attached to a human being, has to be attached to a particular time and a particular place

whereas

The poem, or the kind of poem we write nowadays, is a single emotional spear point

and so

... it is harder to write a good novel than a good poem.[5]

What is common to both forms is the importance of human feelings, and in much of Larkin's poetry these *are* firmly anchored to particular people and places: he may have ceased to write novels but his criteria for the genre became the foundation of his later verse. His last three collections easily pass one of his tests for fiction which his two novels might have failed – 'If I could read it, did I believe it?'[6]

Clearly, the years between 1943 and 1950 were experimental and formative for Larkin. Most artists, particularly writers, take time to discover and develop their individuality – for poets, it might be called finding their own voice. A part of this process is frequently a period spent writing in styles borrowed from other writers. Many writers do not get beyond this stage, and those that do often look back wryly at their early efforts. In T. S. Eliot's view, 'immature poets imitate; mature poets steal'[7] – that is, inexperienced writers need a model from which to work whereas more mature artists make a more considered, conscious use of others' writing.

Much of Larkin's early writing was 'copying': we have his own word for it that as a schoolboy he wrote prose pieces modelled on Virginia Woolf and poems which reflected his reading of the nineteenth-century English Romantic poets.[8] Later, his models were contemporary writers and in an Introduction to *The North Ship* written twenty years after first publication he gives an

interesting account of influence on his early work. He finds in the
poems

> . . . not one abandoned self but several – the ex-schoolboy, for whom
> Auden was the only alternative to 'old-fashioned' poetry; the
> undergraduate, whose work a friend affably characterized as 'Dylan
> Thomas, but you've a sentimentality that's all your own'; the
> immediately post-Oxford self, isolated in Shropshire, with a
> complete Yeats stolen from the local girls' school. (p. 8)

It is not difficult to find these cast-off identities in the collection
(published in 1945), which contained the poems Larkin had
contributed to an anthology *Poetry from Oxford in Wartime*
(edited by William Bell, published in 1944). In 'Conscript', Auden
is clearly present:

> The ego's county he inherited
> From those who tended it like farmers; had
> All knowledge that the study merited,
> the requisite contempt of good and bad; (p. 16)

The narrative tone is Auden's, as is the use of abstractions like
'good' and 'bad', while the application of a geographical metaphor
to the psyche resembles these lines from the sixth of Auden's
'Sonnets from China':

> Falling in love with Truth before he knew Her,
> He rode into imaginary lands,
> By solitude and fasting hoped to woo Her,
> And mocked at those who served Her with their hands.[9]

But more representative of *The North Ship* are these lines from
poem 'XVIII', where the speaker sees grief in terms of the fire he sits
before:

> And I stir the stubborn flint
> The flames have left,
> And grief stirs, and the deft
> Heart lies impotent. (p. 30)

Here we note the presence of Yeats, and perhaps Dylan Thomas too
(in his way, a Yeats descendant). It is not just that, as with many of
the poems in *The North Ship*, there is a strong but unfocused
feeling and a mention of 'the heart'; there is also a fundamental
similarity in the rhetorical style, a calculated use of repetition and
rhythm to produce a song-like effect. Poem 'XVIII' bears a certain
resemblance to Dylan Thomas's 'In my Craft or Sullen Art': in both
the speaker describes a solitary nocturnal struggle with feelings or
poetry, using similar vocabulary – 'night', 'grief', 'heart' – words

both abstract and emotive. Larkin's generalised sadness is also present in *The North Ship*, but in a rather vague way; in *The Less Deceived*, this feeling is always rooted in a specific situation. Only a few poems have titles and in reading them one is often more conscious of the presence of 'the poet' than of the subject, as, for example, at the beginning of poem 'XVII':

> To write one song, I said,
> As sad as the sad wind
> That walks around my bed,
> Having one simple fall
> As a candle-flame swells, and is thinned? (p. 29)

Interestingly, Larkin's friend Kingsley Amis has admitted that he was disappointed by the publication of *The North Ship* and said that he preferred the Audenesque poems about everyday things (never published) which Larkin wrote in his youth.[10]

It will be useful to look at a poem in detail at this point – the final poem in the collection, 'XXXII' (p. 48), comes as a surprise. Please now read it – how does it differ from others?

DISCUSSION

For a start, it is a poem rooted in a specific situation. The first stanza describes someone looking out of a hotel window, using recognisable detail and culminating in a memorable conclusion:

> Drainpipes and fire-escape climbed up
> Past rooms still burning their electric light:
> I thought: Featureless morning, featureless night. (p. 48)

There is a clarity of expression and a firm grasp on language in contrast to the generalised imprecision of phrases like 'the sad wind' in the poem quoted earlier. Furthermore, this poem is not simply about a mood – it has a graspable theme and is recognisably 'about something'. What would you say that 'something' is?

DISCUSSION

It is clearly about a conflict between the woman described in the first two stanzas and a rival:

> . . . Are you jealous of her?
> Will you refuse to come till I have sent
> Her terribly away . . . .

Who or what is this rival? I would suggest that it is the poetic muse
or inspiration and that this is a poem about writing poetry. The
person or thing addressed is described as possessing 'grace', a word
with a number of meanings, one of them theological. 'Grace' in this
sense depicts a gift, an inspiration by God and this idea is taken up
in the final line when the speaker describes himself as

> Part invalid, part baby, and part saint?

Note, incidentally, the characteristic word-play here on '*in*valid/
in*val*id'.) the poem may seem simple at first sight but its inner
meaning is not entirely accessible and could even be thought
obscure. Nevertheless, it delineates a real conflict felt in personal
terms and the 'I' in this poem sounds like a real person, not
someone playing the part of the poet.

In several ways, poem 'XXXII' is characteristic of the poems
Larkin was to write in succeeding years. There is the structure: two
stanzas setting the scene in detail and describing an event (reflection
followed by the kiss); followed by a final stanza where the thought
is brought to fullness in a kind of coda. There is also the exact use
of vocabulary and word-play as in the line

> Fallow as a deer or an unforced field

where there is a pun on the species of deer known as the 'fallow
deer'. And then the narrative voice, the 'I', sounds much more like
that of the speaker in, say, 'The Whitsun Weddings'. None of this is
surprising, for Larkin has explained in his 'Introduction' to *The
North Ship* that this poem was, in fact, written a year or so after
most of the collection and, as he wryly comments, 'though no
noticeably better than the rest, shows the Celtic fever abated and
the patient sleeping soundly' (p. 10).

The 'Celtic fever' is, of course, the influence of Yeats, though
only the Yeats up to 1933 and 'Words for Music Perhaps', for this
was where Larkin's edition stopped. He had been brought to Yeats
by Vernon Watkins who, in 1943, visited the Oxford English Club
and

> swamped us with Yeats until, despite the fact that he had not nearly
> come to the end of his typescript, the Chairman had forcibly to apply
> the closure. As a final gesture Vernon distributed the volumes he had
> been quoting from among those of us who were nearest to him (p. 9)

This episode had a profound effect on Larkin who then

> spent the next three years trying to write like Yeats, not because I
> like his personality or understood his ideas but out of infatuation
> with his music . . . (p. 9)

Another aspect of the early Yeats which Larkin does not mention but is discernible in the two novels written at this time is his concern with people who are dreamers and see dreams as superior to reality, disastrously so in John Kemp's case. It is arguable that there is an element of Yeats in Larkin, especially in poems which have been described as 'symbolist' in their way of working, but the attempt to be another Yeats came to an end when he discovered the poetry of Thomas Hardy. Larkin explained what he liked about Hardy in a radio talk:

> ... when I came to Hardy it was with the sense of relief that I didn't have to try and jack myself up to a concept of poetry that lay outside my own life – this is perhaps what I felt Yeats was trying to make me do. One could simply relapse back into one's own life and write from it. Hardy taught me to feel rather than to write – of course one has to use one's own language and one's own jargon and one's own situations · and he taught one as well to have confidence in what one felt.[11]

It was from Hardy that Larkin learned to create specific situations in which *focussed* feelings of a strong but simple kind could be described. One of the problems with *The North Ship* collection, the vagueness of the emotions, could be put down to the fact, as Larkin put it, that he really 'had nothing to write about'.[12]

Through reading Hardy, Larkin came to formulate and define his own views on the kind of poetry he admired, which included the work of Christina Rossetti, William Barnes, Wilfrid Owen, Stevie Smith and Sir John Betjeman. From the reviews he wrote of work by these poets, it is easy to see the features in common he admires – accessibility, formal simplicity, traditional forms, and a particular kind of melancholy. Until his death, Sir John Betjeman was, in Larkin's view, the best English poet of our time, an opinion reflected in the amount of space he gave to his work in *The Oxford Book of Twentieth-Century Verse*. Like Larkin, Betjeman saw poetry as an emotional rather than an intellectual business and he believed that 'a direct relation with the reading public could be established by anyone prepared to be moving and memorable'.[13] In the course of explaining what he admired and considered important about Betjeman, Larkin was equally explicit about what he disliked and considered had been detrimental to the writing of poetry, and it can be summed up in one word – 'modernism'. Betjeman

> ... is against the kind of poetry this century has made its own. He has written and created a taste for comprehensible poems in regular metre ...

and

[his] chief significance . . . as a poet is that he is a writer of talent and intelligence for whom the modern revolution has simply not taken place. For him there has been no symbolism, no objective correlative, no T. S. Eliot or Ezra Pound, no rediscovery of myth or language as gesture, no *Seven Types* or *Some Versions*, no works of criticism with titles like *Communication as Discipline* or *Implicit and Explicit Image – Obliquity in Sir Lewis Morris*.[14]

Betjeman is thus important not simply because he is a good and popular poet but because he has achieved this by bypassing the 'modernist revolution'.

Larkin's objections to 'modernism' have become legendary and he expressed them forcefully and wittily both in interviews and in his prose writing. He objected to the demands modernist art makes:

I think a lot of this 'myth-kitty' business has grown out of that, because first of all you have to be terribly educated, you have to have read everything to know these things, and secondly you've got somehow to work them in to show that you are working them in.[15]

Some of the blame perhaps lay with Pound and the notion that 'culture' could be swotted up and it may be that this idea was partly responsible for Larkin's strong 'local' or provincial feeling, that one should stick to what is habitually known and not got out of books. But the figure most accused by Larkin was T. S. Eliot, for it was he 'who gave the modernist poetic movement its poetic charter in the sentence "poets in our civilisation, as it exists at present, must be *difficult*." '[16] Poetry which is not only 'difficult' but deliberately so will fail to establish a proper relationship between artist and reader and, besides being impenetrable in itself, is likely to make the art the prerogative of the academic and the student, neither of whom was among Larkin's favourite readers:

I hate the idea that . . . poetry is to be studied rather than enjoyed, that poetry-reading is a duty of the intellectual and all that. I believe a poet has to enjoy writing poetry and the reader enjoy reading it, or they are both wasting their time.[17]

The element of pleasure is not just a matter of enjoyment but is closely related to the value of the poetry, for

. . . if a poet loses his pleasure-seeking audience he has lost the only audience worth having . . . and the effect will be felt throughout his work. He will forget that even if he finds what he has to say interesting, others may not. He will concentrate on moral worth or semantic intricacy. Worst of all, his poems will no longer be born of the tension between what he non-verbally feels and what can be got over in common word-usage to someone who hasn't had his experience or education or travel-grant, and once the other end of his rope is dropped what results will not be so much obscure or piffling (though it may be both) as an unrealised, 'undramatised' slackness, because he will have lost the habit of testing what he writes by this particular standard. Hence, no pleasure. Hence, no poetry.[18]

It was, incidentally, on these grounds that Larkin lost his early admiration for W. H. Auden whose work after 1939, in his view, became over-literary and out of touch with common speech and experience.

For Larkin, then, poetry is a matter of emotion and pleasure-giving and it has three stages: the first is 'when a man becomes obsessed with an emotional concept to such a degree that he is compelled to do something about it'. The second stage is constructing a 'verbal device that will reproduce this emotional concept in anyone who cares to read it anywhere, any time', which leads to the third stage, 'the recurrent situation of people in different times and places setting off the device and recreating in themselves what the poet felt when he wrote it'.[19]

Part of the 'verbal device' is 'metre and rhythm' which act as a 'means of enhancing emotion'. The implication of this view is that technique becomes secondary, and Larkin admitted that

> the kind of poetry I've enjoyed has been the kind of poetry you'd associate with me . . . on the whole, people to whom technique seems to matter less than content, people who accept the forms they have inherited but use them to express their own content.[20]

By 'technique' Larkin meant a 'new' or 'different' technique rather than skill or craftsmanship, for however 'simple' his view of poetry may seem, he took a proper pride in the art, as his own unobtrusive mastery of a chosen traditional way of writing makes evident.

These reflections post-date Larkin's initial success with *The Less Deceived* and they are those of a man who has found his true writer's identity after a period of moderate experimentation. Did this discovery mean that further changes were not to be expected? As I have already mentioned, Larkin expressed some scepticism about poets 'developing' (which he saw as a modern preoccupation beginning with Yeats) and said that he has wanted simply to become better at what he was doing. Whether there were significant changes in his work over the years is a question to bear in mind through the following chapters. Larkin's view of poetry seems remarkably straightforward, but in recent years some commentators have begun to question his dismissal of 'modernism' and his disengenuous disowning of any knowledge of 'foreign poetry' which he undoubtedly read in his youth and which, as we

shall see, is clearly present in his own work. Nor is Larkin's own
poetry without its difficulties. Mostly he is accessible and the
manner is always direct but there are poems which require careful
unpicking – 'If, My Darling' (*The Less Deceived*, p. 42) is an
example and will not make much sense to a reader unfamiliar with
the writing of Lewis Carroll.

Larkin's talents and qualities are very much his own and he
cannot be contained within a category or school. None the less, he
has often been written about, to some extent, as one of a group of
writers in the post-war years known as 'the Movement'. (Others
were John Wain, Thom Gunn, Kingsley Amis, Donald Davie, D. J.
Enright.) The name 'the Movement' came from a leading article in
The Spectator (1 October 1954), anonymous at the time but now
known to have been written by the literary editor J. D. Scott, which
attempted to describe the characteristics of a new generation of
poets:

> It is bored by the despair of the Forties, not much interested in
> suffering, and extremely impatient of poetic sensibility, especially
> poetic sensibility about 'the writer and society'. So it's goodbye to all
> those rather sad little discussions about 'how the writer ought to
> live', and it's goodbye to the Little Magazine and 'experimental
> writing'. The Movement, as well as being anti-phoney, is anti-wet;
> sceptical, robust, ironic. . . .

Whether there really existed any such thing as 'the Movement' is
much debated. Blake Morrison in his book *The Movement* argues
that it did, and that it was central to the writing of the 1950s.[21] He
sees certain characteristics common to 'Movement' writers –
realistic description, a pronounced interest in the audience,
scepticism related to the philosophy of Logical Positivism, a degree
of cautious self-qualification, respect for traditional forms. Some of
these qualities are evident in a poem by Kingsley Amis, 'A
Bookshop Idyll'. What kind of audience, on the evidence of this
first stanza, would you say he is assuming?

> Between the GARDENING and the COOKERY
>   Comes the brief POETRY shelf;
> By the Nonesuch Donne, a thin anthology
>   Offers itself.

Surely, an educated reader, familiar with the insides of bookshops,
who will know that 'the Nonesuch Donne' refers not just to the
works of the poet John Donne but, more specifically, to the
Nonesuch edition? Indeed, one might even say it's addressed to the
academic reader. This is seldom true of Larkin's poems, even when
they (rarely) contain esoteric allusions. Many of Amis's poems, like

his novels, take a rationalist, sceptical attitude to life; Larkin is rationalist too (in the sense of being anti-religious) but there is a pessimism based on the awareness of death and a fatalistic undercurrent which is his alone among this group of writers. Take 'Next, Please' (*The Less Deceived*, p. 20) as an example, with its final, memorable image of death)

> Only one ship is seeking us, a black-
> Sailed unfamiliar, towing at her back
> A huge and birdless silence. In her wake
> No waters breed or break.

Nevertheless, as the precise, clear expression and detail in this strongly metaphorical stanza show, Larkin's early work did have qualities in common with other 'Movement' poets who, generally speaking, were reacting (in the way of literary history) against the writing of the 1940s – Dylan Thomas and the 'Apocalyptics'. Larkin disputes that he was doing this and explains his change of style on the grounds that 'when you start writing your own stuff other people's manners won't really do for it.'[22] In the same conversation, he also stated that he had no sense of belonging to a group with definable aims, though others beginning to write at the time, such as Amis, were friends. The simple fact is that Larkin's was by far the greatest talent of that 'group', so it is hardly surprising that his work, in its singularity, was both part of the 'Movement' and yet beyond it.

By the time *The Less Deceived* was published (by subscription by the Marvell Press) in October 1955, Larkin's course was set. The writer who began by imitating Virginia Woolf and who set out to be a novelist was, at the age of thirty-three, in due course to become a best-selling and much loved poet.

4. *The Less Deceived*

Larkin had intended to call his first important collection 'Various Poems', about as unstriking a title as could be found, but he was persuaded to change it by his publisher, George Hartley at the Marvell Press. Larkin eventually settled on *The Less Deceived*.[1] The poem the phrase comes from is 'Deceptions' and it is based on an account of the seduction of a drugged child prostitute (in Henry Mayhew's *London Labour and the London Poor*, 1851). The poem concludes with the narrator of the incident, as it were, addressing the child in a sentence both poignant and paradoxical. As the drugged victim who will not discover until she wakes what has happened, the child might appear to be more 'deceived' than the man who raped her, and yet she is actually 'less deceived' because he thought, mistakenly, that he would find satisfaction through his action. (The actual phrase is fairly clearly an inversion of Ophelia's remark to Hamlet 'I was the more deceived', *Hamlet* III i). The words have a specific, comparative meaning in the poem, but evidently it appealed to Larkin as a title for the volume because of its wider application to human experience. That is, it could refer to those who have suffered in some way, and who have relinquished or been made to relinquish their illusions. Illusion and disillusion are related to 'truth' and 'reality' and as Larkin told Ian Hamilton in conversation, he supposed he always tried to 'write the truth'.[2] What he means by 'truth' may become clearer from the poems themselves. Before looking at a selection (my choice), can I suggest that you read the whole volume through, not spending too much time on one poem but forming an impression of its general characteristics? Is it true that all the poems express melancholy, or is there more variety? Then, you might choose five or so poems to represent the range of the volume and, at the end of this chapter, compare your choice with mine that follows.

Would you now read 'Wants' (p. 22). You might ask yourself these questions:

1 What is the poem about?
2 How do syntax and other elements in the writing bring about the feelings expressed in the poem?
3 Does 'Wants' remind you of any other poems in *The Less Deceived*?

DISCUSSION

It seems to be expressing a basic human desire to escape from life and awareness:

> Beyond all this, the wish to be alone . . .

> Beneath it all, desire of oblivion runs.

both sentiments being repeated at the end of the first and second stanzas. In the first, the speaker desires solitude in spite of all the social and, it is implied, artificial alternatives. In the second, this wish and the activities of others are interpreted as concealing a wish not to exist, and customs and rituals, all associated with the passing of time, are seen as evasions from this 'truth' about the human condition. The impression of weariness and the futility of trying to escape are brought out by the use of unrhymed lines and repeated syntax suggesting lassitude ('however we follow . . .' 'However the family . . .') and by the way in which each stanza is framed by the reiteration of a bare statement. Note, too, how the activities of other people are referred to: 'printed directions of sex' and 'tabled fertility rites' suggest not only a mechanical view of intimacy but also a deliberate distancing from others (emphasised by the calculated impersonality of phrase).

Is the pessimism of this poem intended to convey a whole attitude to life? It could be argued that it expresses only a particular mood and that Larkin's thought is altogether more tentative than my account might suggest. But the sense of being diminished by the passing of time and of the absence of future promise are themes which are to be found in many poems from the collection: in 'Next, Please', (p. 20), life's failure to deliver the 'cargo' of happiness is expressed in an extended metaphor of a ship which proves finally to be only a bearer of death (see quotation on p. 55). 'Triple Time' (p. 35), a reference to past, present and future, reflects on lost opportunities and lack of achievement, and in 'Absences' (p. 49), the speaker looks at the sea and realises his own ephemerality in contrast with it, and celebrates the idea of 'oblivion' in the last line.

In all these poems, there is a strong sense of the speaker as an individual voice even though not present in the first person, as he is in 'Reasons for Attendance' (p. 18).

Please now read 'Reasons for Attendance'. Has the poem anything in common with 'Wants'? And are there any differences? Ask yourself these questions:

1 What is the poem saying and what is the meaning of the title?
2 What kind of person is the speaker?
3 How does a choice of verbs determine the mood of the poem?
4 What are the meaning and effect of the last two words?

DISCUSSION

In both poems, the speaker is an 'outsider' who looks at others taking part in social activities or rituals, but there is also a contrast – 'Reasons for Attendance' develops from a particular event rather than from a feeling. The scene is set in the first stanza:

> The trumpet's voice, loud and authoritative,
> Draws me a moment to the lighted glass
> To watch the dancers – all under twenty-five –
> Shifting intently, face to flushed face,
> Solemnly on the beat of happiness.

The rest of the poem amounts to the speaker's justification for what he believes his own life to be compared with what he imagines that of the dancer is. Against the tug of the dance and the intimacy of relationships (significantly reduced to instinctual 'sex') is set the call of a different kind of life, to self-expression through art. Seen this way, the poem's title has a double significance: it refers not only to whether one should be at the dance but also to one's whole reason for being alive, one's *raison de'être*. (In this justifying of existence through the practice of art, the poem is reminiscent of John Kemp in *Jill*). What is presented is 'justification' rather than 'argument' and the mood of the poem has a quality of uncertainty and defensiveness reflected in the verbs ('so I fancy', 'believing this').

How do we see the speaker? His tone seems to me almost blustering, that of an older man who has missed opportunities and who is bluffly determined not to see it as a loss.Notice, for instance, how the 'wonderful feel of girls' (hinting at lasciviousness in the observing speaker) is set against the derisive 'they maul to and fro' to produce a comic ambivalence. One critic, David Timms, sees this poem as an exercise in ironic self-dramatization by Larkin and describes him as playing 'academic university Librarian, just old enough to feel out of touch with the students with whom he deals'.[3]

What do you make of the phrase 'that lifted, rough-tongued bell'? Timms sees it as a reference to Larkin's own work and the particular form of phrase as calculated to expose the pomposity of the speaker. This may be so, but isn't there also behind the humour a genuine and serious reflection on the choices individuals can make in life, ending in a deliberately inconclusive way? Neither being an individual nor 'going with the group' is clearly endorsed; Timms's comment also assumes that 'the speaker' is Larkin: from various comments he has made, it is probably true that this is a quite personal poem, but even to characterise the person as a University Librarian adds detail which is not in the poem and so alters (perhaps distorts) one's perception of the meaning.

Larkin has explained[4] why the poem ends with the devastating qualification 'Or Lied'. These two words are intended to correct any false impression of certainty, and this ambiguity, the 'built-in' comment, is an inverted contribution to 'truth' by questioning, unmasking people's assumptions. They produce an effect also found in 'Wants' (p. 22) – the implication that possibly neither way of life produces real happiness. The distinct conclusions which are logically arrived at in the final stanza are given emphasis by using caesuras and the only complete rhymes in the whole poem.

Let us now turn to another pair of poems from the collection of a different kind, 'Maiden Name' (p. 23) and 'No Road' (p. 26). Consider these questions:

1　What *sort* of poems are they?
2　How would you describe the fundamental technique in 'No Road' employed to develop the thought it expresses? And how is rhythm used to good effect in 'Maiden Name'?
3　What is each poem about?

DISCUSSION

If a category has to be chosen, they are both love poems, though that may seem a strange term to apply to 'No Road' which is about the end of a relationship. In this poem (already referred to in Chapter 2), the breakup is powerfully and precisely visualised through the elaboration of a metaphor, a technique common to a number of poems in this collection. (The use of an elaborated metaphor or 'conceit' to combine thought and feeling is a characteristic of the work of John Donne and other 'metaphysical' poets admired by 'Movement' poets). In the first stanza of 'No Road' the decisiveness of the break is envisaged in terms of a barrier of bricks and trees:

> Since we agreed to let the road between us
> Fall to disuse,
> And bricked our gates up, planted trees to screen us,

The metaphor is skilfully handled and works on two levels simultaneously – as an account of the relationship and as an actual description so that the transition in the second stanza to the idea of 'walking that way tonight' is effortless and natural. The suggestion that it is autumn ('leaves drift'), the death of the year, contributes just as naturally to the end of the relationship.

As well as being about a relationship, the poem is also about wider issues – the effect of time and the degree to which people control their own lives. In the final, paradoxical stanza, the speaker finds a freedom in being an *observer* of the world which is being formed by impersonal time. His non-intervention brings him a satisfaction (i.e. 'fulfilment') but also a sense of his failure or malaise ('my ailment'), a trenchant piece of self-criticism. The thought here is distilled and complex and adds an additional dimension of metaphysical paradox to what begins as a gently sad lyric. Several poems in this collection end in this way, among them 'Toads' (p. 32) and 'If, My Darling' (p. 42), a surrealistic account of the speaker's mind in symbolist style, and they qualify to some extent the assumption that Larkin's poetry is always easily understood.

'No Road' has another quality associated with the 'metaphysical school' of poets (though not exclusively theirs) – it combines thought with feeling. The regular stanzaic form and rhyme reflect the meditative nature of the thought which is given life by a movement in feeling (towards a final resolution), producing an entirely natural transition from the second to the final stanza. The feeling itself is both melancholy and stoic, but part of the retrospection is a degree of tenderness which entitles it still to be called a 'love' poem, and also the sense that the relationship, though over, is *not* dead.

'Maiden Name', though less complex, has the same quality. Like 'No Road' a retrospective meditation, its predominant theme is also time and memory. The speaker is exact about the difference between past and present – how the one continues, in a changed form, into the other. When he is musing on the girl's name, the clarity and precision in defining the distinctions in the question-

and-answer movement from second to third stanza is particularly striking:

> . . . Try whispering it slowly.
> No, it means you. Or, since you're past and gone,
>
> It means what we feel now about you then:

The whole poem displays an apparently effortless elegance and lightness of diction which is the result partly of using rhyming couplets ('abbacca') and partly of a flexible use of iambic pentameters. (For example, a dactyl is used in the first word of the poem, 'Marrying', to establish immediately the relationship of the title to what follows: and, in the second line, the spondee in 'five light sounds' echoes the sense, followed by the third line settling into an appropriately 'graceful' movement.) And the language is a skilful blend of 'spoken' ordinary usage and a more 'poetic' kind.

The attitude to time in this poem is both nostalgic and pessimistic, for there is a contrast between the delight in the memory of the girl and the slightly distasteful attitude to her as she is imagined to be in the present. Since marriage, she is 'depreciating luggage', no longer 'unfingermarked', an adjective applying to more than the letters or other bric-à-brac. How would you describe this feeling, and what kind of reaction might it evoke in the reader?

DISCUSSION

Beneath the accomplished surface of this poem, there seems to me to be strong, even crude emotion, mixing nostalgia with revulsion to produce a disparagement which some readers, especially women perhaps, could find offensive. It is as if the woman's beauty and perfection can exist only in the past, and is thus protected from the unsatisfactory present.

Now take a look at 'Latest Face' (p. 41) which is also about a man's (rather complex) feelings about a woman. In the first stanza, he wonders at her beauty which is for his delight alone, but in the second he has disturbing intimations of what 'real untidy air' will do to his feelings. In the last stanza he wonder whether this 'latest face' will overwhelm him or whether denial of his feelings will lead to madness – strong feelings again. This same sense of distance is present in other poems about women – look at 'If, My Darling' and 'Lines On A Young Lady's Photograph Album'. Frequently the girl's attractiveness is described as 'grace', an appropriately elegant term for an attitude to women which might seem more appropriate to an *objet d'art* than a person. This somewhat aesthetic attitude to women might smack of chauvinism to some readers (however politely phrased), though a more sympathetic interpretation might see it as another aspect of Larkin the dreamer, constructing worlds more ideal than the real.

In these poems the past is static and cannot change; it is the present and the future which are uncertain. The unsatisfactory present is the starting point for a humorous but disillusioning look at alternatives in 'Poetry of Departures' (p. 34). Please now read it and consider:

1 What is the poem about?
2 What conclusion is drawn in the final stanza?
3 Why is it called 'Poetry of Departures'?
4 What devices does Larkin employ to make the poem humorous?

DISCUSSION

I see this as a witty yet serious poem about a man's very ordinary, perhaps humdrum life. It begins with a contrast drawn between the speaker's present life ('I detest my room') and an imagined alternative ('*He walked out on the whole crowd*'). He reflects on his tedium, made bearable partly by means of an imaginary rebellion and partly by an exercise of intelligence rather than of feeling – that is, by first imagining a different kind of life, and then judging it not only as unreal, but unreal in the same way as his present life. But the final irony is the realisation that the alternative existence can be accounted for in just the same stereotyped way as his present life. It would be 'artificial' and

> Such a deliberate step backwards
> To create an object:
> Books; china; a life
> reprehensibly perfect.

The 'nut-strewn roads' he imagines himself treading are the equivalent of his present possessions, for both are equally predictable and, as such, can be seen as objects. The adjective 'perfect', used with some irony in the second stanza to describe the order of the present life, is picked up again in the final line but used pejoratively: the way of life is reprehensible because it is open to the same criticism as the fantasy alternative. The unreality of the alternative is conveyed by the cartoon strip style in which it is described (emotive clichés in the third stanza, caricature in the final stanza), but it actually begins in the first stanza with

This audacious, purifying,
Elemental move.

For those polysyllabic adjectives in Larkin's 'high' style produce a full, steady rhythm redolent of certainty and approval for something which is probably only true in the imagination. This is where the meaning of the title becomes relevant: the illusion of being able to leave unsatisfactory reality for a better, liberating alternative is pretty, artificial and unreal – what many consider poetry to be.

The unreality is particularly brought out by the use of clichés. How does Larkin work this kind of colloquial reported speech in the texture of his poems?

DISCUSSION

Here it is a natural complement to the essentially conversational style of the poem. Larkin manages to contain the clichés within a recognisable form by abandoning regular line length and, for the most part, rhyme, but keeps a careful control over the basically iambic rhythm and introduces full rhyme only at the end of each stanza to pull the preceding lines together. This full rhyme, especially in the final stanza, reflects ironically on the artificial 'perfection' of each of the two ways of life. Larkin introduces colloquial speech into his verse for various purposes: here it serves as a kind of Aunt Sally, comically expressing stock actions and sayings which are then exposed as mere fantasy.

All the poems considered so far have, in some way, expressed doubt, scepticism or disappointment but Larkin is not unrelievedly a poet of gloom. A poem like 'Coming' (p. 17) shows a different, not so familiar, lyrical side of Larkin. Would you now read 'Coming' and ask yourself:

1 What sort of poem is it? How would you describe it?
2 What is distinctive about the language and use of metaphor?
3 How is it different from the other poems we have looked at?
4 What is the effect of the absence of rhyme?

DISCUSSION

It might be called a 'nature poem', and in a way, it is, since it directly celebrates the lengthening evenings, the coming of spring and birdsong, but its real subject, as in most 'nature poems', is the mood and feelings of the speaker. The first descriptive half of the

poem is really a preparation for the final lines, the speaker's
spontaneous pleasure in the scene where he feels

> . . . like a child
> Who comes on a scene
> Of adult reconciling

Qualities seen in other Larkin poems are present – lucidity, spare
but telling choice of detail and, particularly characteristic, highly
original choice of certain words as striking as they are immediately
appropriate. For example, the bird's song is described in a vivid
metaphor as 'fresh-peeled' suggesting that the music is like fresh
fruit (a peeled apple?) – a striking use of synaesthesia. The song is
then imitated in the repeated line about the coming of spring.
(Larkin uses this effect rarely.) Here, the repetition neatly divides
the poem into scene and speaker.

The unfolding of the speaker's mood is unobtrusively
suggested by using conjunctions in the last eight lines to form into
one sentence. The mood itself remains uncertain, as the simile of a
child and his feelings in the enigmatic world of quarrelling adults
suggests, and yet, unlike 'Reasons for Attendance', there is no final
'doubling-back' effect and the final impression, if cautious, is single
and positive. The image of 'adult reconciling' suggests a world
normally unfriendly (more is implied than simply the end of
winter), and the lines characterising childhood as a 'forgotten
boredom' seem gratuitous.[5] We should not, of course, assume that
'I' equals 'Larkin' because this is a poem, a lyric, and not a
reminiscence in verse. Nonetheless, even within the fictional 'I', this
reference does not contribute to the poem – indeed, it is a
distraction, an irrelevance, and sounds a sour note. The dominant
mood of the poem, however, is one of emerging harmony (hence,
perhaps, the title) and this is what makes it unusual. The absence of
rhyme contributes to the sense of the poem gradually unfolding and
opening out. For direct contrast, you might read 'Spring' (p. 36) in
which the very celebration of the season serves to make the speaker
aware of his own desiccation. When the natural world figures in
Larkin's work, it is often associated with the inevitability of death
and decay, and the tentative happiness of the speaker of 'Coming' is
not often found, though another example of this type of poem (and
one where, again, repetition is used) is 'Wedding-Wind' (p. 15),
which expresses the joy of a newly married girl.

Several of the poems we have looked at so far begin with a
scene or an incident which is then expanded into a statement. As
Larkin has said:

I tend to lead the reader in by the hand very gently, saying that this is the initial experience or object, and now as you see it makes me think of this, that and the other and work up to a big finish – I mean that's the sort of pattern.[6]

A particularly good example of this kind of structure is 'Church Going', one of the best known poems in *The Less Deceived* (p. 28). Would you now read it carefully, and then try to answer these questions:

1 What statement is the poem making, and what is the significance of the title?
2 How does structure contribute to this?
3 How do we perceive the speaker? Are there any apparent contradictions?
4 How does precise use of language make the poem memorable?
5 Why do you think this is such a popular poem?

DISCUSSION

I would suggest that the title is a play on words with three meanings

(a) 'going into churches' – like this visit;
(b) 'the church is going' – religion dying;
(c) 'going to church' – as people used to, and as they will in future.

The poem is, then, about religion, its place in people's lives and the places where it is practised. Its basic assumption is that Christianity is a dying religion ('when churches fall *completely* out of use' – my italics) and that there will be an inevitable evolution in people's thinking. The power exercised by religion will pass to other activities. After belief, there will be superstition with 'dubious women' (i.e. 'not respectable', but also 'doubting') acting irrationally (stanza 4), but then 'superstition, like belief, must die'. After 'disbelief', churches will serve only a 'purpose more obscure'. What is this 'purpose'? At this point, the argument which has been clear and certain becomes indeed obscure though no less certain: belief in a supernatural religion is no longer tenable but there remains in humanity a need for seriousness in which to clothe (to borrow the metaphor) 'our compulsions'. What are these 'compulsions'? They are 'marriage, and birth, and death', for the latter two experiences at least are biologically inescapable, and, by being described as 'destinies', they are given meaning and thus purpose, though not one that can be spelled out, and this is the sense in which the argument is 'obscure'.

In the final stanza, the place of the church in people's lives, past and present, is recognised:

A serious house on serious earth it is,
In whose blent air all our compulsions meet,
Are recognised, and robed as destinies.

Because the dignity and mystery of human life is so clearly
recognised in the poem, it has often been asked whether it has any
'religious' or perhaps 'neo-religious' quality. Larkin asserted that it
was 'entirely secular' in its attitudes and, within his definition of the
term (for it is clear that 'divine superveillance' as he terms it[7] is
never contemplated) it seems to be so. (Indeed, the earthbound
quality of the poem is emphasised by the use of the term 'dead one'
(stanza four) rather than 'ghost' which could imply a supernatural
dimension.) Larkin has never publicly associated himself with any
group but the term 'Humanist' seems the appropriate term here in
describing the concluding lines.

What was your analysis of the structure? It is by far the longest
poem in the collection and in using a formal, stanzaic pattern
perhaps shows the influence of both Yeats and Auden. I see the
poem as having three parts: the first two stanzas record a specific
visit to a church and are set in the dramatic present tense.
(Incidentally, Larkin did reveal that the poem was based on a visit
to a church in Northern Ireland,[8] so the 'Irish sixpence' is perhaps
not as insulting as it might seem.) The person's attitude seems
ambivalent – deliberately casual in the reference to God and
'stuff/Up at the holy end' and yet revealing 'awkward reverence'.
The second part comprises stanzas 3–6 and is in a prophetic mode:
the speaker 'much at a loss' speculates on what will become a
religion and its houses. Will some be kept as museums and the rest
left to deteriorate? And who will be the last person to visit the
church as a church? Will it be a 'ruin-bibber' or 'Christmas-addict'
(Perhaps implying drug addition and romanticism) or the present
visitor's 'representative', bored yet irresistibly drawn to the place?
'Uninformed' is an interesting adjective which, by transference,
must apply to the speaker himself. He clearly isn't uninformed in
the usual sense, knowing about 'plate and pyx', so perhaps here the
word is being used to mean 'not accepting' i.e. not 'informed' with
what the place proclaims? Or is it that, as with 'brass and stuff' in
stanza 1, he is deliberately dissociating himself from the place? In
the sixth stanza, we seem to be back in the church (final line) and
this is the beginning of the explanation as to why he often stops to
visit a church which 'is not worth stopping for'.

The final stanza forms the third part of the poem and is a
peroration, a rhetorical conclusion. Look carefully at the language
here – how does it differ from preceding stanzas?

DISCUSSION

In place of the colloquial ('brass and stuff') and the derisive ('one of the crew'), the language becomes earnest and dignified – 'serious' is used three times and links with 'wise' 'robed' and 'gravitates'. (The latter is a brilliant play on words – 'graves', 'grave' i.e. solemn; '*gravitas*' i.e. weight, seriousness – all these connotations linger around the primary meaning.) The rhythm also changes in these final lines, becoming firmer, more stately, for the questions asked in earlier stanzas are replaced here by declarations in Larkin's 'high' style.

What are we to make of the person making the declarations? How does he present himself to us? I have already noted a certain ambivalence in his attitude to being in the church. Does it amount to more than ambivalence, to contradiction perhaps? Is the person playing the preacher in stanza 2 convincingly the same as the rhetorician in the seventh? Some critics have seen an unbridgeable gap between the two but I find Larkin's own comment on the poem – 'I think one has to dramatise oneself a little'[9] – helpful, for it indicates that the poem shows the acting out of a process of thought, a process in which the particular parts are given emphasis to make them distinct. If the poem is an honest exposition of Larkin's own feelings,[10] there is every reason why it should contain apparent contradictions for in this it reflects a common state of human emotions. You may feel, however, that art demands a tidier presentation and that a poem should be better resolved. Personally, I find the honesty of the statement poignant, which is not to say that I agree with it.

I drew your attention earlier to the 'precise use of language' and have already commented on one or two words. Did you spot others which particularly struck you? These are those I noticed: 'echoes snigger' (stanza 2) sounds as though it's the wrong way round ('sniggers echo'?) but in fact there is, of course, no actual laughter, only the suggestion of it. Then, in stanza 3 'chronically' – through the ages – also manages to suggest decrepitude, as 'dubious' in stanza 4 combines 'questionable' with 'doubting' in the most economical way. In stanza 6, 'ghostly silt' is a memorable way to describe a deposit of belief in a supernatural religion, albeit unflattering, as is the phrase 'accoutred frowsty barn' to describe the church. If you consult the *Oxford English Dictionary*, however, you will find that the adjectives are very precise: 'frowsty' means 'musty' which accords with stanza 1, and 'accoutred', in addition to meaning 'equipped', probably derives from '*à coustre*' meaning a sacristan, an appropriately ecclesiastical undertone. Larkin's work is full of phrases like these that stick in the mind long after the particular poem to which they belong has been read and digested and they represent a highly selective, disciplined and distilled use of language.

Now to my final question – *why* is this poem, which has been criticised especially for its final stanza and for the divided nature of the person presenting it, for containing inconsistencies and irresolutions, so popular? One obvious reason is that, as we have seen, it is very accomplished verse. In addition, it is consciously serious in a way that no one has difficulty in recognising and, in expressing experiences and impulses common to many people, it appeals to an uneasily secular age. It also claims, implicitly, to reflect the attitude of that age. Unlike many poems in which Larkin speaks from a solitary experience, in 'Church Going' he takes it upon himself in the second part to speak for a civilisation ('What shall *we* turn them into', 'Shall *we*', '*our* compulsions') and to embody a contemporary public attitude. I think it is probably one of the poems that prompted people to write to Larkin and his publisher saying that they saw their own experiences unforgettably recorded in it.

'Church Going' is, in its own terms, very much a poem about being 'less deceived' – about actually going to places of worship, and also about the impossibility of denying the important part of life that took place within them. The poem's careful distinctions and precise exposition are true of all those in *The Less Deceived*. Many poems in this collection centre on the poet/ *persona* and his reflections and the title aptly suggests this focus. I point this out because in Larkin's second collection, *The Whitsun Weddings*, the emphasis shifts in an interesting way.

In this chapter, I have tried to give some idea of the range of Larkin's work in his first major collection. How did your selection compare with mine?

5. The Whitsun Weddings

The Whitsun Weddings was published to much acclaim in 1964, yet a common critical observation was that Larkin had shown little sign of 'developing' since his last collection. A. Alvarez, himself an author of 'Movement' poems, commented that

> there are no poems here which would look out of place in The Less Deceived and as that was published nine years ago one might say that Mr Larkin was consistent to the point of being static.[1]

Before looking at particular poems in detail, would you now browse over the collection, not stopping too long over any particular poem, to see whether you think Alvarez is right? And you might look, too, for any evidence of change in poetic technique.

DISCUSSION

It is true that *some* poems in *The Whitsun Weddings* explore themes to be found in *The Less Deceived* – 'Take One Home For The Kiddies' is compassionate about animals in the same way as 'Myxomatosis'. But others are quite different – 'Naturally the Foundation will Bear Your Expenses' (p. 13), serio-comic verse, is something new, and 'Self's the Man' (p. 24) is in the same vein. In fact, there is altogether more humour, albeit somewhat bleak in character, in this second collection. There are also more poems which, like 'Church Going', could reasonably be classed as autobiographical, and the title poem is a good instance of these. 'Dockery and Son' (p. 37) is another, and it too has an amusing, anecdotal quality. Generally speaking, I would argue that there are fewer 'difficult' poems in *The Whitsun Weddings* and that is because mostly they are rooted in specific situations, centred more

on people and close observation. None has the abstract quality of
'Absences' (*The Less Deceived*, p. 40) or the relative obscurity of
'Dry-Point' (*The Less Deceived*, p. 19). As regards technique,
Larkin's command of language seems (unobtrusively) even more
masterly, and perhaps more relaxed in this collection, especially in
the longer poems, one of which we shall be looking at closely.

Would you now look at one of the 'serio-comic' poems, 'Naturally
the Foundation will Bear Your Expenses' with these questions in
mind:

1 How is it both serious and comic? Are the two aspects reconciled?
2 What attitude is implied towards the speaker? How are we
   encouraged to see him?
3 What features of language strike you?

DISCUSSION

The speaker is a 'jet-setting' English academic about to leave
London for Bombay to deliver a paper previously given at the
Berkeley campus of the University of California. He is thinking how
it may also be used for a talk on the BBC Third programme (as it
then was) before being issued as a book by the London publisher,
Chatto & Windus. The title is presumably intended to be
characteristic of the kind of invitation such a person would receive
– 'Foundations', more familiar in North America, (e.g. the Ford
Foundation) award funds for travelling scholars. (The commercial
associations of the funds are perhaps approrpriate to the multiple
uses the 'pages' are to be put to.) Then, airborne, the academic
reflects on the Cenotaph Remembrance Day service which delayed
him on the way to the airport and dismisses it derisively.

What makes this poem different is that it is funny in a way
quite unlike any other Larkin poem published before, and yet at the
same time, as he himself pointed out, it is 'as serious as anything I
have written'.[2] Some readers, have found it hard to reconcile the
humorous style of light verse with a serious intention. Colin Falck
took Larkin to task, asking

> Should we really, in this post-Nazi age, be dismissing 'solemn-
> sinister wreath-rubbish' in a piece of light verse?[3]

Another wrote of Larkin's style in this poem as 'rollicking
Betjemanesque' (the rhythms and the use of commercial, everyday
names are certainly similar), with the implication of 'lightweight'.[4]
Yet most jokes are, or can be, intrinsically serious.

There are several kinds of humour in the poem (e.g. there is the use of abbreviations, satirical at the speaker's expense), and the prevailing mood is ironic. The irony lies in the gap between the sentiments of the speaker who assumes a sympathetic listener and the probable reactions of the reader, for surely we are intended to deplore his dismissal of Remembrance Day? I think this is evident from the poem, but there is some biographical corroboration. Explaining to Ian Hamilton how the poem came about (*Twentieth Century* magazine asked for something for a Humour number), Larkin was rather casual about having heard the Remembrance Day service on the radio – 'happening unexpectedly' on it.[5] Introducing the poem on a recording of *The Whitsun Weddings*,[6] however, he said that it was in fact his habit to listen ('I usually do'), which suggests that he probably cared more about the service than he chose to admit. The seriousness of the poem lies in the hostility of the speaker and his contemptuous dismissal of the Service, an event which Larkin and the majority of British readers in 1961 respected (whatever reservations some intellectuals may have had), as 'solemn-sinister/Wearth-rubbish' and the poem relies on this for its effect.

The poem is also serious in its implied condemnation of the 'middleman' speaker and his attitude to literature. Larkin's dislike of a certain type of academic who uses books to produce his own commodity was well-known. The knowing reference to 'Morgan Forster' i.e. E. M. Forster (the one-time representative of a humane liberalism) is singularly inappropriate.

As to language, the clause 'dwindle down the Auster' is another example of Larkin's use of exact, uncommon words, for Auster, besides providing a rhyme, is mediaeval English for 'South Winds' or 'South', the direction in which he would have been flying. (The term survives in 'Australia'.) Also, in the familiar metaphor at the end of the first stanza, there is an echo of the well-known passage from St Paul's Epistle to the Corinthians:

> When I was a child, I spake as a child, I understood as a child, I thought as a child: but when I became a man, I put away childish things. For now we see through a glass darkly;* but then face to face.
> *[Or, in a modern translation, 'puzzling reflections in a mirror'.]
>
> (*Corinthians* I, 13 11–12)

The echo of these lines in 'darkly/Through the mirror of the Third' is much to the point as Paul's message is about charity in all its forms (noticeably absent in the speaker). He likens the attainment of understanding to the growth of a child to adulthood and this is just what, in the final stanza, the speaker by implication characterizes *himself* as having completed:

O when will England grow up?

The echo of St Paul adds to the irony, and a full reading of the poem depends on grasping this. Some readers seem to miss this or, if they do not, find it difficult to accept a shocking irreverence set in a comic context. Fundamentally, correct interpretation depends on determining the type and function of the persona which varies from poem to poem. The poet is always present in some sense (however obliquely) and distinguishing between him and his persona is especially delicate in lyrical poetry, and almost all of Larkin's work if of this kind. The poet's own attitudes and ideas (which are likely to be reiterated throughout his or her work) can be inferred but only by paying close attention to tone and diction. Failing to do this is surely responsible for the mis-readings that have arisen with this poem whereby a certain kind of intellectual is seen as 'unpatriotic' and sympathetic to the very position Larkin is satirising.

'Naturally the Foundation' is a new kind of poem for Larkin in another way – it is a satirical poem on a *public* theme. There is nothing in *The Less Deceived* like it, though there are others that follow in *High Windows*.

Let us now turn to the title poem of the collection. Would you read it, paying close attention to the tone, and ask yourself

1 Does it show any new qualities? Of observation? Of language?
2 How would you describe its technical characteristics?
3 What the attitude to the weddings is? How is the narrator involved in them?
4 What the last six lines mean and how they should be read?

DISCUSSION

The new feature is its length, equalled by no previously published poem. Related to this is its leisurely character – it recreates in its own rhythms the length of the journey it describes. The principal subject, the wedding parties, is not introduced until the third stanza; the beginning of the poem is devoted to evoking the smells and sights which flash past an observer in a moving train and these everyday, commonplace landscapes are described with a novelistic particularity:

           . . . We ran
Behind the backs of houses, crossed a street
Of blinding windscreens, smelt the fish-dock

The same attention is paid to the details of dress that follow:

> The nylon gloves and jewllery-substitutes, the perms,
> The lemons mauves, and olive-ochres . . .

As David Timms has pointed out,[7] Larkin makes a new use of the 'ready-made' language of advertising which economically produces two effects – adding realism and, at the same time, socially placing people by describing their clothing.

In technical terms, the poem consists of eight ten-line stanzas set in an impressively regular rhyme scheme 'ababcdecde'. The metrical unit is the iambic pentameter, sometimes of Shakespearean eloquence ('A slow and stopping course southwards we kept'), at others almost banal ('At first, I didn't notice . . .'). The remarkable thing is the variety Larkin achieves while keeping strictly to this metre throughout this long poem (excepting the second line of each stanza). This impressive feat of verbal embroidery is not immediately evident when the poem is read aloud, for the conversational style of diction tends to obscure it. Precisely because it is a leisurely account in colloquial style, the technical precision of expression is all the more necessary as a backbone for the patterned verbal construct we call a poem.

The attitude towards the weddings is not altogether easy to establish, for there seems to be a distinction between the 'marriages' described at the end of poem and the 'weddings' in the middle. Larkin has been accused, and perhaps with some justice, as snobbish and patronising in the description of the latter. Undeniably, phrases like 'seamy foreheads', 'mothers loud and fat ' and 'parodies of fashion' suggest the superior, solitary observer recording with deadly accuracy that the gloves are *nylon* and the proceedings as a whole more than a little vulgar. ('Whoops and skirls' and an 'uncle shouting smut' suggest tipsiness, and fathers enjoying success 'wholly farcical' is very double-edged i.e. they are making others laugh and are wholly laughable in doing so.) Each wedding itself is seen as possessing a catalytic quality, bringing out in children, fathers and women their own kind of involvement in the ritual. The reaction of these participants to weddings is described in arresting phrases which precisely describe their feelings. The girls staring 'at a religious wounding' is a particularly striking observation.

Social ritual clearly interested Larkin and the detail of the description in this poem shows close observation. Does it also show genuine interest in the lives of ordinary people, or is the narrator simply a condescending observer? John Wain believes that, although solitary and apart, he participates by and through his recording of the event:

> . . . such contemplation – rapt, unwavering, emphatic – is a way of 'joining in' and the only way that art knows. The poet contrasts the essentially self-preoccupied mood of the young couples with his own sense of involvement in a moment of complicated multiple experience.

This contrast, Wain shows, is evident in the distinction in the penultimate stanza between 'none/Thought' and 'I thought'. Paradoxically, he concludes that

> the poet's involvement is greater than theirs; he sees and understands just what it is that each participant feels, and then puts them together to form one complete experience, felt in its directness by no one, yet present in the atmosphere and available to the imaginative contemplation that makes 'art'.[8]

The 'experience' Wain refers to, the 'travelling coincidence' and the meaning it contains, is brought out in the final stanzas, in particular the last six lines.

> The human situation in the train
> Stood ready to be loosed with all the power
> That being changed can give. We slowed again,
> And as the tightened brakes took hold, there swelled
> A sense of falling, like an arrow-shower
> Sent out of sight, somewhere becoming rain.

Most of the poem, Larkin has said, should be read on a 'level, even a plodding, descriptive note' but these 'mysterious last lines . . . should suddenly "lift off the ground"'.[9] In writing them, he had 'the sense of a kind of simultaneous arrow shower and rainfall' which, he reluctantly admits, 'was, I suppose, deeply symbolic in various ways'.[10] Each couple, the 'arrow-shower' image suggests, will set off in their own direction, and the ending of the journey is really a beginning for those on board. The ritual over, there is a movement towards a new growth, subtly suggested by the notion of 'swelling' and rain falling. The idea of fertility has been introduced in the previous stanza in the description of London's postal districts 'packed like squares of wheat' where, Larkin says, he was aiming at conveying both 'overcrowdedness . . . but also fruitfulness'. (In the first draft, he had written 'fields of wheat'.[11]) This is an unusual effect, for the notion of change in Larkin's work usually means deterioration.

The poem ends on a positive note, even, one might say, with a suggestion of transcendence: something new will grow out of these weddings and the people will be changed. Larkin achieves this effect by powerful and subtle images – 'arrow-shower' is especially striking because it combines the force and strength of a projectile with the notion of wide dispersal and gentleness. This technique is not frequently found in his work but its presence here does much to substantiate the suggestion that in some ways Larkin remains a poet occasionally employing symbolist techniques, and one in whom Yeats still lives.

Talking about the poem, Larkin commented:

> I've always said that this is one poem anyone could have written; you simply had to sit in a railway carriage and see what went on, and write it down afterwards.[12]

He later qualified this remark on discovering from the manuscript that it had taken him two years to finish, with many alterations and revisions, but it is, none the less, a disingenuous comment if John Wain is right, as I believe he is. Anyone might have observed the weddings (and perhaps not as patronisingly) but the notion of the 'travelling coincidence' and its diverse vitality is Larkin's alone.

There are other poems in the collection that show a similar interest in the lives of ordinary people. Please now read one of them – 'Here' (p. 9). After reading it, consider these questions:

1 What does the poem describe?
2 How would you describe the point of view, or attitude?
3 What is the subject of the poem, and why is it called 'Here'?
4 How does the final verse differ from the first three?
5 What do you notice about the rhyme scheme?

DISCUSSION

Like 'The Whitsun Weddings', 'Here' is again about a journey on a train (as the 'halt' indicates) and the movement of it is cleverly caught by the repeated use of the participle 'swerving' to describe its progress through the countryside. The second verse describes the train's destination ('Gathers' implies a terminus later confirmed by the adjective 'terminate') which is a large docks town with an estuary river (presumably Hull). The second and third verses then give a description of the town and its inhabitants, some of whom live outside it on 'raw estates' and are lured to it by the shops and the material goods they have to offer

> Cheap suits, red kitchen-ware, sharp shoes, iced lollies,
> Electric mixers, toasters, washers, driers

(The phrase 'by stealing flat-faced trolleys' does not mean theft but

that the trolleys are enticing, seducing people to the stores.) Then, a
contrast is introduced as the scene changes to wheat-fields and
subsequently (final stanza) to a beach. The method is cinematic.
One scene dissolves into another, each vividly described. It is a very
highly observed poem and works through its detailed account.

Where 'Here' differs from a film is that we see everything
through the eyes of the narrator who, though apparently detached,
is not indifferent to what he sees. The description of the town's
inhabitants as a 'cut-price crowd' might sound condescending for it
implies that *they*, rather than the goods they pursue, are cheap with
all that that implies. I don't think this is the case because it is
qualified by 'urban yet simple, dwelling/Where only salesmen and
relations come' (i.e. no tourists) – 'urban' is a neutral term and
'simple' in this context is complimentary. Nevertheless, a clear
distinction is drawn between the observer and the observed: the
latter flock to the town to go 'to *their* desires' (my italics) while the
narrator comes to his.

It is the final stanza that reveals the poem's subject and
explains the title. Using verbs in the present tense, the narrator
conveys an immensely powerful awareness of his own 'unfenced
existence', glorying in his solitude. It is the opposite of a lifeless
state – all the verbs are associated with growth ('thicken' 'flower'
'quicken') and the air itself is 'luminously-peopled' (i.e. alive with
lights). As the lines 'where removed lives/Loneliness clarifies'
indicate, solitude and quiet generate a purity of existence – the
construction is inverted and in prose would run 'loneliness clarifies
removed lives'. The effect of the inversion is to put the stress on
'clarifies'. In the same way, 'Ends the land suddenly' is also an
inversion.

This unusual syntax emphasises the immediate situation in this
final stanza, its concentration on what Larkin calls in another poem
'the million-petalled flower/Of being here' ('The Old Fools', *High
Windows*, p. 19). The final stanza is given a specific location –
weeds, poppies, a sea shore – but the discourse is deliberately more
abstract than the earlier verses, for the obvious reason that it is
exploring an abstraction, the mystery of being. In this way it is
different in kind, and this is reflected in the way language is used –
three sentences begin with the demonstrative form 'Here . . .'.

There are two rhyme schemes – stanzas 1 and 3 share one,
stanzas 2 and 4 the other, thus

'ababcddc abbacdcd ababcddc abbacdcd'

My point in drawing this to your attention is to illustrate again that
Larkin frequently employs what is, on examination, a surprisingly

complex form of traditional methods in a poem which initially
seems straightforward.

'Here', 'The Whitsun Weddings' and 'Faith/Healing' (p. 15) might
be grouped together as poems in which Larkin observes the lives of
others, lives quite different from his own. His life is solitary, other
people's are crowded. Is this just honest reporting (and painfully
honest)? Or does the contrast carry a judgement, so that solitude is
generally the superior state? Fairly clearly, Larkin simply values
solitude in itself, but is there perhaps implicitly snobbish
withdrawal from group life? Or is there a bit of both? With this
question in mind, I suggest you look now at a poem which deals
with people like himself – that is, with his interests and education.

Would you please read 'Dockery and Son' (p. 37)?
   Consider these points:

1 What has it in common with 'The Whitsun Weddings'?
2 What is the subject of the poem, and what is its meaning?
3 What comment would you make about *diction*?
4 Do the concluding four lines seem an appropriate conclusion to the
    poem?

DISCUSSION

It seems reasonable to assume that, as in 'The Whitsun Weddings',
Larkin is speaking *in propria persona* i.e. in his own voice (he was,
in fact, twenty-one in 1943 and still at Oxford, though this is of
biographical rather than critical interest.) Also the narrator is again
on a railway journey – being on the move gives him a literal as well
as a metaphorical detachment and both poems unfold gradually
through a reported narrative.
    The poem recounts a return visit to the speaker's old college
and his thoughts about his contemporaries. The first stanza
provides an excellent example of the compactness of Larkin's
powers of description in calling the speaker 'Death-suited,
visitant'. The phrase suggests three different meanings: 1 that he is
wearing a dark suit as for a funeral occasion; 2 that he is a ghost
returning ('visitant' = *revenant*); 3 that 'death suits him'. The
appropriateness of the last suggestion becomes apparent when the
poem reaches its conclusion. Unlike 'The Whitsun Weddings' with
its final, positive image, this conclusion declares unambiguously that
life is frustrating, determined, hard, meaningless and leads only to
death. (Finding the door to his old room locked is a potent image of
the irrecoverable past.) The highest beliefs and ideas 'warp

tight-shut' and the 'innate assumptions' which are 'all we've got'
appear in the harsh, arid image of sand-clouds as an impenetrable
barrier to attaining anything different. The final lines of the poem
are uncompromising indeed:

> Life is first boredom, then fear.
> Whether or not we use it, it goes,
> And leaves what something hidden from us chose,
> And age, and then the only end of age.

The speaker reaches this conclusion by comparing Dockery's
life with his own. The railway lines on his way home (third stanza)
and the 'joining and parting' of the railway lines suggest a
predetermined course for his and Dockery's lives (an idea
strengthened by the mention of the 'strong/Unhindered moon' with
its astrological associations). The possibility that Dockery has
consciously chosen his course in life is considered and then rejected;
his life, like the speaker's, is seen as the inevitable outcome of his
'innate assumptions'. The title, besides being a reflection on the
implications of fatherhood, suggests the image that Dockery has of
himself – that his identity is formed by his rôle. And there is an odd
sort of joke: 'Dockery and Son' sounds like a business, not to
mention the hint of the nursery rhyme 'Hickory Dickory Dock',
with the suggestion of time recorded mechanically by a clock.
    Seeing parenthood as a 'dilution' of the self might seem
defensive and suggests that the narrator's actual existence might be
challenged by being involved in procreation. But, with unflinching
honesty, he goes on to say that the alternative (which is all *he* has)
amounts to 'nothing', a fact which mocks him as much as a son
would have done:

> For Dockery a son, for me nothing,
> Nothing with all a son's harsh patronage.

As Larkin was himself a childless bachelor, it seems likely that this
was rather a 'personal' poem.
    The diction seems to me particularly interesting in its diversity.
The poem has three different modes. First the one-sided
conversation in a dramatised incident: in Larkin's own recorded
reading of the poem, the Dean's words

> 'Dockery was junior to you,
> Wasn't he?' said the Dean. 'His son's here now.'

– are delivered in a squeaky, mimicking voice which makes him a
figure of fun. In the second stanza the diction modulates into the
second reflective mode as the speaker thinks back, and this

gradually develops into the third, the assertiveness of the final lines, the 'coda' already quoted.

Larkin once called final perorations of this kind his 'strong second act curtains'[13] but one might ask whether it is an appropriate image for 'Dockery and Son'? Is the lapidary statement of the conclusion integral to the poem, or has it been tacked on as the answer to a question which has not really been raised? It does not seem as integral to me as, say, the conclusion of 'The Whitsun Weddings' where the final image relates directly to all that has been described. On the other hand, if you see this (as I do) as an intensely *personal* poem, then the concluding statement might be justified simply by the fact that it *is* what the poet's reflections lead him to.

But 'Dockery and Son' is not unrelieved gloom. As well as the initial lines there are other humourous flashes – the vignette of hung-over undergraduates explaining their misdeeds, the joke about railway catering ('an awful pie'). This combination of pessimism and humour is an interesting feature of Larkin's work. He has a vivid awareness of human mortality. 'Nothing to Be Said' (p. 11) insists that all societies, primitive and modern, are overshadowed by the inevitability of death so that every human action becomes part of dying. For those aware of this sombre fact, there is, says the poet, no consolation.

In some poems, this grim consciousness of human suffering is combined with humorous observation to striking sardonic effect. 'Sunny Prestatyn' (p. 35) is an example. Would you now read it and ask yourself:

1 Do you find it both funny and serious? If so, how?
2 If you do find it funny, how would you describe the humour?
3 Does there seem to you to be another, less immediately accessible emotion in the poem?
4 What is your reaction to the language, and what is Larkin's purpose in writing this way?

DISCUSSION

Whether or not you find it funny will depend to some extent on your sense of humour (and also, perhaps, on your reaction to the language used) but surely the sorry state the poster is reduced to and the bawdiness of its despoliation is at least intended to amuse? It is, in a way, like the humour in the plays of Joe Orton – funny and outrageous, deliberately drawing attention to what you may choose not to see ordinarily. It is difficult to explain *why* something is funny without killing it, but surely the wry attitude to the poster is amusing? The inanimate paper girl is 'slapped up' and yet she 'laughs a welcome', just as advertisements relate to life and yet are quite misleading images of it, and this is the serious comment the poem is making. The paradise portrayed is unreal –

> She was too good for this life.

And so the advertisement is replaced by one proclaiming harsh reality:

> Now *Fight Cancer* is there.

So the laughing frozen image of happiness in the first stanza is replaced by the stark reminder of pain and death in reality (and *this* poster will, presumably, remain unmarked.) As Larkin himself remarked:

> Some people think it was intended to be funny, some people think it was intended to be horrific. I think it was intended to be both.[14]

The poem suggests through resigned irony that advertisements are essentially delusory and that finding or keeping beauty in real life is not possible.

I would call the humour 'wry' – variously oblique and indirect. The poster itself is risible:

> Come to Sunny Prestatyn
> Laughed the girl on the poster,
> Kneeling up on the sand
> In tautened white satin.

This is emphasised by the deliberate use of a weak rhyme 'poster/coast a'. (Larkin explained, incidentally, that the poem's origin was 'one of those jolly, colourful posters that are so beloved by the publicity officers of seaside towns showing the universal symbol of happiness, a pretty girl.'[15]) Then there are the added scrawls which, if bawdiness is to your taste, will raise a smile. Such pornographic additions, familar to everybody, are described in accurate and memorable detail and the reader's attention is focused on them, whereas, in reality, most would simply glance and look away. The effect is heightened by another kind of humour in the ironic addition of the autograph. (It's not necessary and rather literal-minded to see 'Tich Thomas' as a real person.) So the reader is lead to a wryly new awareness of posters like the one described.

But is the humour concealing or holding in check another, concealed emotion? Do we sense that 'Sunny Prestatyn' is on the edge of another feeling, one of anger perhaps that reality is *not* like the paradise advertised? Perhaps this feeling is not *strongly* present, but it is explicit in others we shall come to, so it is worth considering here.

Did this poem initially shock you? It does many, perhaps less by the explicitness of detail than by down-to-earth language. You might well think that words like 'tits' and 'cock and balls' have no place in a serious work of literary art, by a writer of Larkin's stature. Is he trying for a quick, easy effect? Is it perhaps because he wants to emphasise the despoliation of the poster with language to match the handiwork? The words themselves are not especially 'bad' (there are worse) but they are precisely pointed up by exact adjectives like 'fissured', the language of an educated observer, and this acts as a foil, one setting off the other. And could Larkin have achieved his aim *without* being so direct? Probably not, and the contrasting language both sets off and offsets the vulgar. (You might note, too, that the poem was first published *after* the obscenity case against Penguin Books had been lost over the publication of D. H. Lawrence's *Lady Chatterley's Lover* in its unexpurgated form.)

In *The Whitsun Weddings*, 'Sunny Pretatyn' is one of several poems about advertisements: what their claims and exaggerations have to do with real life clearly fascinated Larkin. Would you now look at 'Essential Beauty' (p. 42) and consider:

1 The significance of the title.
2 The relationships between the people and objects depicted in the advertisements and the boy, the pensioner and the smoker in the second half of the poem.
3 What emotions do you sense (remembering my earlier remark about concealed feeling?

DISCUSSION

I think the title fairly clearly refers to the Platonic notion of essences, which is applied to the impossible perfection of life as pictured in advertisements. The irony of the contrast between the real world with all its dirt and imperfections and the unreal existence depicted in advertisements is highlighted by a rhyme which serves to juxtapose the two:

> ... Rather, they rise
> Serenely to proclaim pure crust, pure foam,
> Pure coldness to our live imperfect eyes

'Coldness' suggests 'uninviting', and by implication 'imperfect' life has a reassuring 'warmth'.

There is, too, a possible second meaning in the title which could be taken as a statement – 'beauty is essential'. Certainly, the figures described in the second half of the poem are seeking unreal and ungraspable forms of beauty, but the boy 'puking his heart out in the Gents' (literally vomiting but also 'losing his heart') will never be with the smart set in their tennis clothes; the pensioner enticed to pay more for her tea gets only the taste of old age; the dying smokers have a sense of a mysterious presence approaching them but it has nothing to do with cigarettes ('No match lit up, nor drag ever brought near'). As with the *'Fight Cancer'* poster, the real world is peopled with the old and the dying 'where nothing's made/As new or washed quite clean' and what is most real in people's lives (in spite of their passion for the beautiful) has nothing to do with the forms of 'beautiful living' that advertisements convince them are essential.

The emotions present in the poem seem to me of several different kinds – there is astonishment at the outrageous unreality of advertising, (reflected in the 'butter/gutter' rhyme) and in the second part of the poem a sadness and compassion for those falling so far short of 'essential beauty'. There is also, perhaps, a tinge of amusement in the way the hoardings are described. But behind these one senses a repressed anger that life does not measure up and is made worse by the promises of duplicit, 'essential' images, and this anger is, as it were, kept at bay by the making of the poem.

The final poem in this 'advertising' group that I would like you to consider is called 'Send No Money' (p. 43). Would you read it, and consider:

1 The point of the title.
2 What kind of poem it is.
3 What happens in the poem.
4 What the final lines mean, and how the sound of them conveys their sense.

DISCUSSION

The title relates to the controlling metaphor of the poem, that 'the truth' turns out to be a 'truss-advertisement', and is the instruction usually attached to small advertisements which offer a 'free trial' before purchase.

The most appropriate way of describing the poem is, surely, to call it a parable, or an apologue? The moral of the tale turns as follows: the poet as a naïve young man seeks to find 'the truth' by waiting for the course of events to reveal a pattern and, meanwhile, refrains from active interference in them, from having 'a bash' (i.e.

at 'life' or even, perhaps, sex). Helped in this by lack of envy ('no green in your eye') he resolves simply to watch life even though Time is teaching him that there is no recognisable pattern. Eventually, his life half over, he recognises that life in a physical world ('the bestial visor', i.e. his own face) is altered by completely arbitrary events ('what happened to happen') which reveal its complete meaninglessness. The indiscriminate and painful nature of events is brought out by the use of a metaphor which is developed in terms of force – others want 'to have a bash', there is a 'clash', occurences 'clobber life out'. His conclusion is uncompromising:

What does it prove? Sod all.
In this way I spent youth,
Tracing the trite untransferable
Truss-advertisement, truth.

The truth promised by Time is like a 'truss-advertisement' because it promises a support and comfort for an injury which in reality it cannot give. There is also the possible hint that Time itself, with an impendent belly, is in need of a truss. 'Truth' is untransferable because it has to be discovered by each individual from experience. The sense of disillusion and angry disgust in these lines is underscored by the alliterative repetition of the spilling consonants 'tr' five times in seven words.

This is an unusually fanciful poem for Larkin, though it has some familiar features (such as the dramatisation, the use of different 'voices'), and the message it conveys, that life is dominated by an indeterminate fatalism, is entirely characteristic. There is another feature of the poem associated with the self-characterisation of the narrator which brings 'Reasons for Attendance' (*The Less Deceived*, p. 18) to mind – look again at the discussion of the poem on p. 36. What might that be?

DISCUSSION

Both poems draw a contrast between the narrator, 'outside' and passive, and others, who are a group and 'active'. Paradoxically, the narrator establishes himself in both poems by conscious non-participation. In a similar way, there is a parallel between the compensating call of 'art' as an alternative to life in the one poem and the commanding wish to be 'finding out' as an alternative to the 'it' others seek in 'Send No Money' – that is 'art/finding out' are in opposition to 'life/it'.

As well as being an 'advertising' poem, 'Send No Money' could also be grouped with those poems whose theme is time. Usually it is seen as a threatening dimension to life – see 'Nothing to be Said' (p. 11) – or as an unsettling bridge between past and present – see 'Wild Oats' (p. 41). On the whole, the past is the safest aspect of 'time' since the present usually disappoints and the future threatens. The past is often seen as a lost, somehow better era. You can see this kind of nostalgia more easily in *The Less Deceived* (e.g. 'Maiden Name', p. 23, or 'Lines on a Young Lady's Photograph Album', p. 13).

But *The Whitsun Weddings* has one poem that embodies it supremely – 'MCMXIV'. Would you now read it, and answer these questions:

    1 What is the unusual grammatical feature of this poem? How does it contribute to the poem?
    2 Does 'nostalgia' best describe the feeling in the poem?
    3 What attitude to history does it imply?
    4 Why is the title in Roman numerals?

DISCUSSION

'MCMXIV' is unusual grammatically in that it has no main verb. Larkin has said that this did not happen by design; nevertheless, the absence of verbs (which are to do with *events*) surely contributes to the deliberately static evocation of a country just before the upheaval of the First World War. What was about to erupt (the War itself) is never actually mentioned, so there is another reason for not having a main verb. Larkin has said that he called it 'MCMXIV' because 'I wanted to remind the reader of a date on a monument and because I felt the emotional impact of 1914 was too great for anything I could possibly write myself[16].) It is an interesting remark, for it reminds the reader that

> Those long uneven lines
> Standing as patiently
> As if they were stretched outside
> The Oval or Villa Park,

include many men whose names were to appear in later years on the monument.
    Larkin's remark also confirms the impression that the society depicted is deliberately set at a distance and dissociated from the present. In that sense, the poem is not 'nostalgic', for the term actually means a 'longing for home'. On the other hand, the attitude to the past, which is seen as flawless, verges on the sentimental. Paradoxically, in spite of the period detail (no licensing

laws, the children's names), the impression built up is somewhat artificial.

Perhaps Larkin intended to create a vision of peaceful innocence but the lines

Never such innocence,
Never before or since,

somehow do not quite ring convincingly, because every reader must know that no period in history is unblemished. Given Larkin's somewhat jaundiced view of his own times and this idealised view of the pre-war era, one might reasonably argue that his view of modern history is that it has been a steady decline.

I would like you now to go back to the question I posed at the beginning of this chapter and consider it again in the light of the poems you have now read. Was A. Alvarez right? Are there no changes in the poems in *The Whitsun Weddings*? I hardly need say that it is not my view. Whether Larkin 'developed' between his second and third collections is perhaps not what matters: what is certain is that *The Whitsun Weddings* contains poems showing a marked increase in range and accomplishment, all recognisably by the author of *The Less Deceived*. If this is 'developing', then Larkin can be said to have done so.

6. *High Windows* and After

High Windows, published in 1974 to much acclaim, was to be Larkin's final collection of poems, though he did publish a few individually in magazines in the following years, one of which – 'Aubade' – I shall be referring to. Would you now do as you did with *The Whitsun Weddings*, read through the collection without pausing too long on any one poem and see whether there are noticeable 'types' of poem? For the purposes of discussion in this chapter, I have put the poems into six groups, most but not all of which we have come across before. Of course, some could belong to more than one category, but it will be interesting to see how your classification matches mine.

My first group I shall call 'observation' poems – that is, poems which depict different lives and customs. A good example is 'Show Saturday' (p. 37). Would you now re-read it, and consider these points:

1 How does the poem progress?
2 How would you describe the pace of the poem?
3 What kind of writing is this?
4 What is the narrator's attitude to the life he observes?
5 Do you think it is a good poem?

DISCUSSION

The principle of progression in the poem is chronological. It follows the course of a single day, the day of the show, from early morning to late evening. But also it proceeds by moving from one 'Show' event to another. Jumping events are followed by wrestling and judging of produce until, the day over,

> ... The pound-note man decamps.
> The car park has thinned.

So, like many of Larkin's longer poems, 'Show Saturday' moves in a leisurely fashion, and the method is basically impressionistic. The piling up of carefully observed detail suggests a narrator wholly familiar with such events. What saves his account from being too familiar to the reader to be interesting are the quirky observations, turning the known into something interestingly new e.g. the bales of straw:

> ... Folks sit about on bales
> Like great straw dice.

or the notion that husbands present are 'on leave from the garden/Watchful as weasels'. Further, the poem is cast into a regular rhyme scheme 'abacdcd' which employs combinations of some ingenuity – 'animals/bales', 'wired-off/pods of' are examples. This rhyme scheme provides a formal and disciplined structure but of an unobtrusive kind suitable to the leisurely occasion of the show. There are no regular line lengths, nor a strictly iambic metre.

The narrator's attitude or 'point of view' only becomes evident in the final two verses. In the first six he has been a neutral observer, panning like a camera over the assembled show. But in verse 7 we begin to sense his attitude to some aspects of the scene. There the families are described;

> Children all saddle-swank, mugfaced middleaged wives
> Glaring at jellies, husbands on leave from the garden
> Watchful as weasels . . .

As in 'The Whitsun Weddings', what interests the narrator are the emotions of those he is observing. Does he see himself as superior to these people? It seems to me that the humour and inventiveness of detail do not give this impression: the wives 'glaring at jellies', presumably in rivalry, and 'saddle-swank' as a way of describing the child's pride in winning the pony event are unforgettable. There is, too, admiration for the *skills* which the competitors display. The final verse is the narrator's evaluation of this annual summer ritual. His comments suggest that it is almost organic, staying hidden (like bulbs in the earth) until the time comes round again for it to break 'ancestrally each year into/Regenerate union'. There is also the darker hint that the people involved in the annual show are mercifully protected from recognising that its regular occurrence points to the inexorable progress of time and hints at 'much greater gestures', i.e. death. 'Regenerate' is an interesting, positive adjective to employ in the final line, while the concluding imperative 'Let it always be there' proves beyond doubt that we are asked to approve the whole occasion, and see this particular social, communal activity as praiseworthy and helpful.

Is it a 'good poem'? I think it is, and I shall admit that, in posing the question I initially had some reservations about its length, the *amount* of detailed observation and the comparative 'neutrality' of the early verses. In the course of writing about the poem, however, these features have come to strike me as quite deliberate and part of its peculiar character, and it is a poem which has grown on me.

The other poems I would group with 'Show Saturday' as 'life observed poems' are 'Friday Night in the Royal Station Hotel' (p. 18), which evokes the atmosphere of a stolid businessman's hotel and the way of life it supports; 'Livings' (p. 13), a tryptich, the first part similar in subject matter to 'Friday Night in the Royal Station Hotel' while the second and third parts describe the lives of a lighthouse keeper and members of a seventeeth- or eighteenth-century Oxford or Cambridge college respectively; and, finally, 'To the Sea', an account of families spending the day by the seaside. The last of these makes a good companion piece to 'Show Saturday': the disposition of the narrator in both seems very similar. In 'To the Sea' he is 'happy at being on my own', watching the families around him on the beach, going through an annual ritual, and, again, the poem ends on a note of approbation that people are

> . . . teaching their children by a sort
> Of clowning; helping the old, too, as they ought.

It's a very different attitude from the man in 'Dockery and Son' who seems to feel he has to defend his single, childless state.

Another poem that might go with this 'observed' group is 'The Card-Players' (p. 23). But it depicts its scene from life in a bizarrely different way, and also seems to me a good deal more complex. So I would allot it to my next group, the 'satirical poems'. Would you now read it and consider these points:

1 Does it resemble any Larkin poem looked at so far?
2 What are its peculiar features, and how does it work?
3 Why is the poem deliberately coarse?
4 How should we read the last line – humorously?
5 How, technically, would you describe the poem?

DISCUSSION

Like 'MCMXIV', 'The Card-Players' has a historical setting: it evokes a scene from the past, but there the resemblance ends. 'The Card-Players' is a verbal *tableau vivant* from a former century, an enactment of an interior scene painted by a Dutch Old Master. This is never actually stated but the names and details ('lamplit', 'ham-hung rafters') strongly suggest it and it is, in fact, an accurate evocation of a certain kind of Dutch genre painting in which people are seen performing ordinary actions. The poem is constructed, however, by a technique quite the opposite of that used in 'MCMXIV'. There we were presented with a series of photographic, frozen scenes. The method in 'The Card-Players' is to bring the painting to life by making its figures move and by giving details, especially of sound, which a painting cannot convey ('croaks', 'snores', 'farts').

It would be a naïve reader who failed to notice that Larkin gives his three card-players names which are a scatological play on words about vomit, excrement and the penis, and the poem begins in a way calculated to bring the reader up short:

> Jan van Hogspeuw staggers to the door
> And pisses at the dark . . .

Is Larkin being deliberately offensive rather than amusing (as with 'Sunny Prestatyn')? There is certainly a lot about bodily functions described in colloquial slang. Is Larkin simply playing the *enfant terrible*? Perhaps he is to some extent indulging in schoolboy humour but as in other 'funny' poems looked at earlier, a serious point is also being made about the relationship between art and reality. (In a similar fashion, 'Essential Beauty' examines the contrast between advertisements – a debased art form? – and life.) Much visual art idealises and presents a picture of static life in which balance, light and colour blend to produce an overall impression which is contained and pleasing. 'The Card-Players' parodies that kind of painting, desanitates and brings it firmly down to earth by providing both the kind of detail to be found in a Dutch Old Master and deliberately crude descriptions of actions not normally thought of as appropriate to 'art'. Especially clever is the effect of Dirk Dogstoerd holding

> . . . a cinder to his clay with tongs,
> Belching out smoke . . .

for 'Belching' both describes the volume of smoke *and* suggests eructation. Could it be that this is conscious iconoclasm? Larkin, you may recall, once said that he disliked a 'false relation between art and life' and one could see this poem as a witty illustration of the point. Possibly, too, Larkin is recalling that both Yeats ('Municipal Gallery Revisited') and Auden ('Musée des Beaux Arts') wrote celebrated poems about paintings – is 'The Card-Players' his own way of doing the same thing?

The calculated crudity can also be explained in another way. Each of the player's actions has a parallel with something in the natural world, and the comparisons are not flattering to the humans: Jan 'pisses' and outside it rains; Old Prijck 'snores' and Jan 'farts' against the wind in the trees. The human and the natural world are brought together in the final line.

> Rain, wind and fire! The secret, bestial peace!

which stresses that the animality of men, however unattractive it may seem, forms part of the natural physical world. The elemental aspect of man is set against the elements themselves (as in *King Lear*). The men themselves, though, find a secret peace in their animal nature because it links them with the elements and they find a reassurance through this.

The last line is perhaps an ironic comment on the foregoing scene and is also a deliberately partial view of human life as a whole. Does it contain a touch of envy for such unthinking existence in the physical world? Envy is an emotion allied to contempt, so the final line is a somewhat ambivalent summary.

The final line in fact performs the function of the final couplet in a sonnet, since this poem formally resembles a sonnet using the Miltonic rhyme scheme in which octave and sestave are not separated.

a	door	c	tongs
b	rain	d	gale
b	lane	d	ale
a	more	c	songs

(The last line of the octave – ending in 'songs' – grammatically runs over into the first line of the sestave.) The scheme of the final lines deviates from the strict pattern but it is certainly recognisable as a variant of the established form. Both in this respect, and in the use of colloquial language, 'The Card-Players' can readily be identified as by the hand that wrote *The Whitsun Weddings*.

Because 'The Card-Players' doesn't easily fit any one category, I would now like you to look at another from the 'satirical' group into which I have put it. Would you read 'Annus Mirabilis' (p. 34)?

1 Why is it called 'Annus Mirabilis' and what is it about?
2 Is it fair to call it satirical, and how would you describe the tone?
3 Do the specific cultural and historical references strengthen or weaken the poem's impact?

DISCUSSION

To realise the full significance of the title, you would need to recognise it as a borrowing from a poem 'Annus Mirabilis' by the English poet Dryden, published in 1667. Translated, the Latin means 'Year of Wonders' or 'Extraordinary Year': Dryden chose it because his poem deals with the victory of the English over the Dutch and the Fire of London. Larkin uses it to pinpoint 1963 as the year when the so-termed 'sexual liberation' began, and he chooses that year in particular because it was three years after the Crown lost its court case against Penguin Books for publishing the unexpurgated version of Lawrence's novel *Lady Chatterley's Lover* with its explicit sexual language. It was also the year before the beginning of the phenomenal success of the pop group The Beatles with all that signified – the start of the 'Swinging Sixties' as the decade was sometimes described. The poem's beginning

Sexual intercourse began
In nineteen sixty-three

startles partly by using the clinical term, partly by its apparent absurdity. It is, of course, an ellipsis – it is really saying that pre-marital sexual relations became acceptable to many, as the second verse makes clear with its reference to a 'wrangle for a ring'.

But evidently the speaker was too old for all of this to affect him. Is he then really envious? I think not, for I sense that his tone is as ironic as the title. There may be a tinge of regret, but stronger is the implied question 'Was it all really so marvellous?'. I think this is evident from the third stanza with its hyperbolic superlatives:

Everyone felt the same,
And every life became
A brilliant breaking of the bank,

Life, as any reader of Larkin's work knows, is not like that, and so I would say that the poem is gently satirising the notion that the 1960s was a time of great liberation.

The specific references slotted colloquially into a formal rhyme and stanzaic scheme are a form of shorthand: the '*Chatterley* ban' makes immediate sense to any reader born in the 1940s or before but, if the poem is still read in fifty years from now, it will need some explanation. This is equally true of the reference to the Beatles, who even now, in the latter years of the 1980s, need to be explained to younger generations as a phenomenon of the popular culture of England in the 1960s and 1970s. In one way, this could be seen as a weakness, but only if you think that poetry should somehow be outside time. In another way, the time-locked references gave readers in the 1970s (for whom, after all, it was written) a great sense of being addressed by someone of their own time, and in this sense the shorthand added to the poem's immediate impact. And, you could argue, the references could well induce the reader to investigate the shifts in cultural history referred to (as Pope's references in *The Dunciad* take us into literary life in eighteenth-century London).

Another poem which tackles the question of 'liberation', though in a more reflective way (which is why I have not put it into this group) is 'High Windows' (p.17). You might care to look at it now, for immediate comparison, though I shall be discussing it later.

Other poems in this 'satirical group' to look at are 'Vers de Société (about time-wasting parties, contrasted with the wish to be alone, p. 35); 'Sympathy in White Major' (a quite complex poem, which employs clichés to demolish the notion that recognised virtue lies in sharing life with others, p. 11); 'Posterity' (a bitterly amusing fictional dramatisation of an ambitious young American academic who is reluctantly writing the biography of the poet, p. 27); and, finally, 'This Be The Verse' (an epigrammatic account of how one generation psychologically wounds the next, p. 30).

As a change from these 'personal' poems, I want now to turn to two poems in *High Windows* which are deliberately 'public'. Perhaps 'two' are rather few to constitute a group, but there are other published poems, not collected in *High Windows*, which belong to this group. One of the *High Windows* pair, 'Going, Going' (p. 21) commissioned by the Department of the Environment, originally formed a prologue to a government report entitled 'How Do you Want to Live? A Report on the Human Habitat' (HMSO 1972). So it is an 'occasional' piece – written to order for a particular purpose. Would you now read it? Would you say:

1 That, although 'occasional', it resembles other Larkin poems in any way?
2 That it is satisfying as a poem?

DISCUSSION

Is it not reminiscent of those poems in *The Whitsun Weddings*, like the title poem, or 'Here', which are imbued with 'Englishness'? As in 'Here', Larkin looks both at urban life and at what lies beyond it and has a clear preference for the 'unfenced existence/Facing the sun'. Between 'Here' and 'Going, Going', however, there is a fundamental change in attitude. On balance, 'Here' affirms a solitary existence in surroundings of rural beauty in contrast with the crowded urban life of ordinary people. Yet the urban scene is accepted as *part* of the total environment, whereas in 'Going, Going' it is an encroaching horror which will eventually obliterate the alternative 'beyond the town', and the very title suggests the finality of a hammer falling at an auction:

> . . . It seems, just now,
> To be happening so very fast;
> Despite all the land left free
> For the first time I feel somehow
> That it isn't going to last,
>
> That before I snuff it, the whole
> Boiling will be bricked in
> Except for the tourist parts –

The speaker identifies himself in the first three stanzas with those who accept the progress of despoliation with resignation; but in the later verses he expresses and elaborates on a newly pessimistic view that greed and the rate of change will overtake his lifetime. The process is roundly condemned as immoral and the cries for 'more' of everything become 'greeds' in this zeugma in the final stanza:

> ... but greeds
> And garbage are too thick-strewn
> To be swept up now

The coming decline is attributed to the work of a 'cast of crooks and tarts' and, while speculators might be seen as 'crooks', it is not so clear where 'tarts' fits in.

'Going, Going' is, then, another poem that sees the future as inevitable decline into something worse than the present. How well does Larkin write this 'occasional' verse? In comparison with his more personally rooted poems, this attempt to combine public and personal does not, perhaps, come off so well. Because it *is* a commissioned, public poem, Larkin is obliged to ensure that his view (which is, after all, not particularly original) is expressed unambiguously and thus unironically too. It lacks his usual certainty of touch in its hesitant self-questioning and, in place of the customarily striking choice of word or phase, the language is rather uninteresting, verging on cliché. Perhaps 'public' poems *should* be more staid in their diction, but nevertheless the style does not display Larkin's gift at its best, while the poem's historical perspective is foreshortened.

I think you will find that the same is true of the companion poem in *High Windows*, 'Homage to a Government' (p. 29), an obviously ironic title. The feeling in the poem seems genuine enough, but the issues involved are but skimmed over and it is a lack-lustre piece of writing. There is a similar limpness about 'Party Politics', an uncollected poem in two stanzas about getting a drink at a party, contributed to a special issue of the *Poetry Review* on 'alcohol and poetry'.[2] One should recall, though, that 'Naturally the Foundation will Bear Your Expenses' was also commissioned, and that is a decided success; the reason for this being that it is *funny*. So too is another successful commissioned piece that Larkin wrote for Gavin Ewart's 65th Birthday, 'Good for You, Gavin',[3] an affectionate piece of light verse, deftly picking up features of Ewart's style. Another unpublished occasional poem that Larkin wrote, 'Bridge for the Living', set to music to celebrate the opening of the Humber Bridge in 1981, is a decided success and convincingly affectionate about Hull, 'her face/Half-turned to

Europe, lovely Northern daughter.' It's when Larkin is being simply dutiful or deliberately serious in his demeanour that things seem to go wrong, which raises the interesting question of what kind of poet laureate he would have made.[4] He was certainly offered the post but turned it down. The reasons are not difficult to guess: he had virtually stopped writing and was, anyway, a very private man. Had he, nevertheless, accepted, one feels that the few poems he would have been called to write in the short period between the new appointment and his death would not have added to his reputation.

Death, as we've seen, is a strong theme in Larkin's writing and he wrote about it constantly and powerfully. We have already looked at some examples (pp. 12, 56). In this my fourth group there are two more examples in *High Windows*, and then one printed in 1977 in the *Times Literary Supplement*. Would you now read the first of the two in *High Windows*, 'The Old Fools' (p. 19)? Then consider:

1 How this poem differs from others you have read on the subject of death.
2 Whether you are shocked by the poem, and if so why.
3 What feelings are revealed as the poem unfolds – are they all directed at the old people?
4 What the poem says about death.
5 How you might describe the form of the poem, and how it contributes to its overall effect.

DISCUSSION

What makes 'The Old Fools' different from earlier poems on this same subject is that ageing and death are not presented as abstractions or generalities but as a terrifying present reality embodied in the senility of geriatric people.

I think the poem *is* shocking, and is meant to be. The title itself becomes shocking as soon as the reader realises to whom it is being applied, for 'old fools' is a term of contempt sometimes applied to elderly, physically able people, and the suggestion that they might be *deliberately* drooling, or drunk, when everyone knows this is not the case, is startling. The poem may even offend some readers and it can hardly be read without discomfort because it forces us to face undignified and humiliating realities about our human condition. If this is your reaction, I suggest that you then examine it in relation to the other feelings and the overall response Larkin is striving to evoke.

The first thing to be said about the emotion in 'The Old Fools' is that it is strong and deep, and changes as the themes of old age and death are developed. The first stanza is built on a series of questions arising from a deliberately harsh description of senility:

> ... Do they somehow suppose
> It's more grown-up when your mouth hangs open and drools,
> And you keep on pissing yourself,

Such lines present an appalled awareness of the reality of old age which combines compassion with deep anger that such a state of affairs exists. This gives way to the flat assertions of the second stanza that death is final, set off by a highly lyrical description of the wonder of life as 'the million-petalled flower/Of being here'. In the third stanza, the mood becomes speculative in an imaginative attempt to realise the experience of being old:

> Perhaps being old is having lighted rooms
> Inside your head, and people in them, acting.

This stanza is especially beautiful in its feelings *for* the old, in contrast to the harshness of the first, yet like the first it leads us into looking at this stage of the human condition in a new way. This attempt to understand an alien condition leads to the conclusion that the old really do inhabit a different world:

> ... That is where they live:
> Not here and now ....

and leads into the final stanza which returns on a desperate note to the questioning of the first:

> ... Can they never tell
> What is dragging them back, and how it will end?

Desperation then turns into grim certainty when the speaker identifies himself with the old people, realising that his question will be answered in time – 'Well,/We shall find out.'

The poem never allows the possibility of dignity in old age. It focuses on the death that will certainly follow, and anger at that fact is its driving force. When the speaker uses such vicious terms as 'as if they were crippled or tight', he is less attacking the old people themselves than the physical reality of old age and death (though there could also be an element of genuine repulsion, honestly recorded). Writing about Betjeman's *Collected Poems*, Larkin noted the more frequent mention of death in the later work and commented:

> Fear of death is too much of a screaming close-up to allow the poetic faculty to function properly, but demands expression by reason of its very frightfulness.[5]

His own view of death is stark and blunt – it is 'oblivion'.
Paradoxically, this uncompromising belief is accompanied by a
vivid awareness of being alive and all these 'death' poems (unlike
earlier ones) express a deep and affecting sense of both life and
death:

> ... It's only oblivion, true:
> We had it before, but then it was going to end,
> And was all the time merging with a unique endeavour
> To bring to bloom the million-petalled flower
> Of being here.

The harsh irony of 'only oblivion' is actually heightened by the
addition of the conversational 'true', then leading to the
extraordinarily memorable metaphor of the flower, to be followed
by others just as striking – the 'lighted rooms' of memory,
'Extinction's alp' facing us all. The declaration that death is final
comes, of course, as no surprise, given the poet's explicit disavowal
of any religious belief. After Larkin's own death, A. N. Wilson
recalled in *The Spectator*:

> Larkin had an absolute conviction that death was nothing but
> extinction. It was a fact which filled him with terror and gloom.
> Religion was completely unable to console him. Last year, he read
> through the Bible from cover to cover. He had a large lectern-size
> Bible and he read it while he was dressing. When he had finished it, I
> asked him what he thought. 'Amazing to think anyone believed it
> was true' was his only comment. Yet many of his closest friends were
> religious and he shared the wistfulness of one of his favourite poets,
> Thomas Hardy, about his inability to believe.[6]

The poems on the subject must therefore be seen as unambiguously
personal, directly stating their author's awareness that

> If you assume you're going to live to be seventy, seven decades, and
> think of each decade as a day of the week, starting with Sunday, then
> I'm on Friday afternoon now ... I dread endless extinction.[7]

The form Larkin chose for 'The Old Fools' is, like some other
poems already examined, both formal yet flexible: an analysis of
the rhyme reveals a regular scheme of some complexity
('abacdedfef') which acts as a 'frame' for each of the twelve-line
stanzas. Against this carefully worked out scheme are set lines of
speech of irregular length which rise and fall according to the
movement of the feeling, from appalled rhetorical questioning to
flat assertion. The rhyme scheme, then, gives the poem a firm shape
while allowing Larkin to operate flexibly in a conversational mode
within the poem, yet introducing wonderfully distilled metaphors
which remain in the mind long after the poem has been read.

The other poem in the collection concentrating on death works exclusively through metaphor. Would you now please read 'The Building' (p. 24)? Consider these questions:

1 What *is* the 'Building'?
2 What are the metaphors on which the poem turns? And what do they signify?
3 How does the poem achieve its threatening quality? How does the rhyme scheme contribute to this?

DISCUSSION

Fairly clearly, the Building is a hospital and the vehicles that draw up at the entrance are ambulances. Stanzas 2 and 3 describe the waiting room and the variety of people in it, all sharing one thing in common – their sickness.

At the same time, the Building is a metaphor for human life in the world and its ills (curiously, in this respect, like Section IV of T. S. Eliot's *East Coker*). But before this is taken up at the end of the poem, another metaphor is introduced in stanzas 5 and 6 where the Building becomes a prison, full of rooms 'And more rooms yet, each one further off/And harder to return from'. In marked contrast, someone is seen outside walking 'Out to the car park, free'. Then in the eighth stanza the Building becomes a kind of church where the patients are 'unseen congregations'. Finally, the religious ideas, previously hinted at by describing the patients as 'Here to confess that something has gone wrong', is taken up and countered in the final stanza. The visitors' flowers are 'wasteful, weak, propitiatory' – useless offerings which will do nothing to help, for there is nothing to suggest that the Building's powers *will* 'Outbuild cathedrals'. So, although religion is explicitly brought into the poem, suffering and death are seen as an entirely secular affair without explanation or alleviation and presented as the human condition. In this sense, 'The Building' is less 'observed' than descriptive and pedagogic in style, and this is evident in the use Larkin makes of the imperative mood – 'see. . .', 'see . . .', 'look down . . .'.

Part of the poem's threatening quality derives from the starkness of its message – 'All know they are going to die' – but it is accentuated by a deliberate indirectness, an obliqueness of description, creating an air of terrifying mystery. Larkin achieves this by using negatives and consciously wrought imprecisions – the vehicles 'are not taxis', the people working there are 'a kind of nurse', 'something has gone wrong'. The rhyme scheme helps him achieve this effect by its very irregularity. There are rhymes within each stanza but, more significantly, they are carried over to succeeding stanzas – take for example stanzas 2 to 4 where you find 'sit/refit', 'although/below', 'caught/sort', 'all/tall'. So, again, rhyme is holding the poem together, yet there is no easily identifable pattern and this is appropriate to its overall mood of undefined threat. Yet, in the midst of its gloom, there is a brief lyrical episode celebrating life beyond the Building:

> . . . O world,
> Your loves, your chances, are beyond the stretch
> Of any hand from here!

and these lines seem to me deeply felt.

The last of the 'death' group 'Aubade' (*Times Literary Supplement*, 23 December 1977, p. 1491.) is, if anything, bleaker in its expression of fear of dying, especially felt when 'we are caught without/People or drink'. In this poem, religion is quite explicitly dismissed as an answer to death:

> . . . Religion used to try,
> That vast moth-eaten musical brocade
> Created to pretend we never die.

But death is the 'sure extinction that we travel to'. Some readers have felt that Larkin's constant turning to this theme and the bleakness of his outlook had a deleterious effect on his work. Would you consider this for a moment?

DISCUSSION

Whatever your own view of death, it's impossible not to be impressed by Larkin's hugely imaginative awareness of it as an experience, and by the compelling honesty of the feelings he records. You don't have to agree with a poem to enjoy it, and Larkin's sheer mastery of language makes reading these poems an engaging, memorable experience. Also, as I have tried to show, the reverse side of this dread of death is an intense awareness of the wonder of life, and it is this which rescues this group of poems from unrelieved negativity.

Sensitivity of this kind lies at the heart of some of the shorter poems in the *High Windows* collection, and these form my fifth group which I call 'celebratory'. Among these is 'Solar' (p. 33). Would you now read it? Ask yourself:

1 What *kind* of poem is it?
2 How might you describe the tone of the speaker, and what is his viewpoint?
3 In what ways does Larkin develop his theme and keep the image before the reader?

DISCUSSION

I would call it a 'paean' – that is, a song of praise to the sun, full of awe and wonder. There is no poem in Larkin's work more visionary than 'Solar', for it celebrates the life-sustaining sun, describing it first in terms of the kind of picture you might find in a child's nursery:

Suspended lion face

Then it moves into scientifically accurate language:

Continuously exploding

(The sun is nuclear fusion, turning hydrogen into helium, tons every minute.) I find it difficult to avoid using the word 'religious' (albeit in a pagan sense) to describe the poem – so might an Aztec or Zoroastrian or other sun-worshippers address the heavenly body.

The tone is surely one of thanksgiving or tribute, and it is achieved partly by using a repeated construction 'How . . . How . . . you exist . . . You give'. There are also echoes of Psalm 103, one verse of which reads in a modern translation:

All of these look to you
To give them their food in due season.
You gave it, they gather it up;
You open your hand, they have their fill.[8]

There is the same form of direct address and the image of a living hand which is 'unrecompensed' – that is, it is benevolent and beneficent. It is interesting, too, that Larkin uses the simile of human needs rising 'like angels' and that he concludes the poem with a declaration of eternity which is reminiscent of the phrase 'for ever and ever'.

These connotations raise, for me, the question whether Larkin is in any sense (intentionally or otherwise) 'religious'. It was a notion he always resisted; but could one not describe 'Solar' as religious in the sense of acknowledging dependence on something external to the self? From another angle, it could be seen as a poem about the universe, for the adjectival title invites the complementary noun 'system'. Indisputably, as Larkin himself admitted, the poem was 'unlike anything I'd written for twenty years',[9] and it does reveal what may be, from one point of view, interesting contradictions in his work. (Another poem with a 'religious' element in it that you might look at is 'Water' – see *The Whitsun Weddings*, p. 20.)

In developing his theme, Larkin is inventive and ingenious in keeping the image of the sun before the reader. In the first stanza, the sun is seen as a flower (reminiscent, perhaps of Van Gogh's painting 'Sunflowers'). Then the idea of *roundness* is transmuted in the second stanza into a head, taking up the idea of a face from the beginning of the poem. This becomes a coin in the final stanza, ingeniously linked to the second by the suggestion of the 'heat' needed to cast it in gold. 'Gold' is an indication of the reciprocity of these qualities and, perhaps, at the same time, a suggestion of a gold coin ringing. The 'lonely horizontals' in which the sun lies are, presumably, the clear horizon, the 'unfurnished sky' of the first stanza.

'Solar' is unusually single in tone and there is none of the irony or ambiguity which is a feature of many of Larkin's poems. The mood is established in the first stanza and then sustained through to the concluding doxology in unrhymed, irregular lines which reflect the free movement of feeling. Pace, too, is established in the first stanza, partly by an abundance of 's' sounds which act as an alliterative brake.

The other poems in *High Windows* that I would group with 'Solar' are 'The Trees' (p. 12), a three-stanza lyric about annual blossoming which, while it mentions death, also sees each year as a new beginning; and the middle part of 'Livings' (p. 14) in which a lighthouse-keeper rejoices in the savagery of the elements.

It cannot be incidental that 'Solar' is placed immediately after 'Sad Steps' in the collection, for one is about the sun and the other, in one sense, about the moon. 'Sad Steps' belongs in my final sixth category which I shall call reflecive. Would you now read it?

1 Why is it called 'Sad Steps'?
2 And what is the subject and theme?
3 How would you describe the diction, and what use is made of rhyme?

DISCUSSION

The feelings and thoughts of a man looking at the moon in the middle of the night form the subject of the poem, and the 'sad steps' of the title refer in the first instance to his making his way back to bed with his reflections. As the sun in 'Solar' is benign, so the moon here is nocturnal and somewhat threatening, 'High and preposterous and separate'. The moon in the night sky embodies strength and, it is suggested, in some sense destiny, like the 'strong/Unhindered moon' and the railway lines which reflect it in 'Dockery and Son'. In a wider sense, the steps are a metaphor for the speaker's inevitable ageing, yet the passing of time and the inevitable approach of old age, a familiar theme in Larkin's poetry, is not viewed in the stark fashion of 'Dockery and Son' because, it is implied, there are compensations. Seeing the moon, and remembering its romantic associations, reminds him

> . . . of the strength and pain
> Of being young; that it can't come again,

Age, that is, brings its own kind of freedom. The title, as in other poems we've looked at, also contains a literary allusion. If you are familiar with the poetry of Sir Philip Signey (as Larkin undoubtedly was), you may recognise the title as a borrowing from the thirty-first sonnet in the sequence *Astrophel and Stella* which begins 'With how sad steps, o Moone, thou climb'st the skies', and Sidney's poem is very much about Cupid the 'busie archer' and the pain he brings.

I can see three kinds of diction in 'Sad Steps'. The poem begins with the colloquial, blunt description of an experience familiar to everyone and then, as if brought up sharp by the night sky, moves through elevation into an ironic apostrophe to the moon

> Lozenge of love! Medallion of art!

which then modulates into the sober conclusion. The whole is woven together through a regular rhyme scheme of 'abb abb aba', and by the steady iambic rhythm.

Another poem which I would put in this group and which also expresses the idea that age brings its own kind of liberation is 'High Windows' (p. 17). Larkin modestly stated that he did not 'think it very good' but that it was a 'true poem'.[10] Would you now read it? What is it 'true' about? What function, if any, does the crudity of the first lines serve?

DISCUSSION

To take the second question first, the poem brings with a deliberately coarse statement about a kind of sexual freedom brought about by contraception, and Larkin admitted that this was intended 'to shock' and such language was 'part of the palette'.[11] I think his purpose in using it here was to underline the ironical comment 'I know this is paradise', for sex described without any reference to feelings of love, even in its cheapened sense, can only be antonymic to the meaning of paradise. The deliberate crudity emphasises the contrast between the two.

The sexual freedom of the young (if ironically presented) is their particular liberation and it leads the speaker on to what he believes a generation before his own would have seen as his – namely, freedom from religious authority.

> No God any more, or sweating in the dark
> About hell and that . . .

And at this thought,

> Rather than words comes the thought of high windows,
> The sun-comprehending glass,
> And beyond it, the deep blue air, that shows
> Nothing, and is nowhere, and is endless.

And so the poem ends with a powerful image of freedom – 'infinity and absence, the beauty of somewhere you're not', as Larkin put it[12] – as distinct from the 'liberation' enjoyed by two different generations of young people. It is a surprising conclusion to the poem and suddenly the diction moves into elegance and elevation, culminating in the final, perfectly harmonious line.

There are, I would argue, several different kinds of 'truth' in the poem. To begin with there is what he sees as a 'series of oppressions'[13] being swept away, first religious and then sexual, so dispelling hypocrisy. Yet, the irony implies, the young couple described are not made happy by their sexual freedom but take it for granted as the speaker does his atheism and this is underlined by showing such 'progress' as a 'long slide', that is, a *downward* movement. One thinks, perhaps of the Gadarene swine in the New Testament, or the psalmist's lines

> How slippery the paths on which you set them;
> You make them slide to destruction.[14]

In contrast, the movement in the final stanza is *upward* to the 'high windows' where the image of infinity (strongly reminiscent of the end of 'Here') suggests a true freedom which is beyond any kind of oppression or liberation.

An interesting feature of this poem is that although it begins from an observation, it is mainly metaphorical and does not depend on the careful working out of an incident, leading to a conclusion. This kind of writing is in some sense *'symboliste'* and Barbara

Everett believes the origin of the windows image to be in a poem by
Mallarmé:

> The radiant colour and the 'nothingness' are too Mallarmean to be
> only coincidentally similar . . . his poetry is full of '*De l'éternel azur
> la sereine ironie*' (the calm irony of the endless blue). The poem by
> Mallarmé in which this image becomes most definitive is 'Les
> Fenêtres (the Windows).[15]

The similarity of the titles makes this hypothesis tempting, but there
could be a much simpler explanation which occurs to most people
who visit the Brynmor Jones Library at the University of Hull
where Larkin worked. It is simply that the most striking feature of
the principal extension to the library (built under Larkin's aegis
there) are a series of windows set very high up on every wall of the
library, and so, remote, static and unchanging. Whatever the origin
of the image, it undeniably hints at some sort of transcendence, in
spite of Larkin's protest 'I don't want to transcend the
commonplace, I love the commonplace'.[16] The two are not, in fact,
necessarily incompatible (though Larkin seems to think so), for the
notion of rising above the ordinary does not necessarily mean
abandoning it.

There are several other poems in the collection which I would
group with 'High Windows' as 'reflective': 'Cut Grass' (p. 41) is a
brief lyric set in summer which touches on death and ephemerality;
'Money' (p. 40), a four-stanza poem with some rather weak rhymes
which ponders the subject of its title; and 'Dublinesque' (p. 28), a
vignette of an Irish funeral procession, ending on a poignant note of
'great sadness'.

I wonder how far your grouping of the poems agreed with
mine? Some of these types of poem can, of course, be found in the
earlier volumes but the general style of *High Windows* seems to me
to be more relaxed and more self-confident. If this is good, as I
believe it is, then it confirms Larkin's aspiration simply 'to become
better at what I am'.[17] When the volume appeared in 1974, most
reviewers agreed that the subjects, if often familiar, had been
developed and clarified – 'reinforced or deepened rather than
repeated', as one put it.[18] Finally, here is Larkin's own view of his
last collection, a way of looking at the poems which you might bear
in mind as you look back over the volume. Asked whether he would
agree that there was more 'compassion and generosity in *High
Windows* as a whole', his answer was 'I should like to think so',
and he went on to add

> . . . I'm glad if you do find the poems in *High Windows* more
> compassionate: I don't know that they are. But one must be more
> aware of suffering as one grows older . . . .[19]

7. Larkin's Achievement

Larkin stopped writing poetry in his later years, although he continued to write book reviews fairly regularly. There has, then, been plenty of time for readers to consider his published verse in its entirety. It is to facilitate this that each of the three major collections has been considered separately and in chronological order. It should be clear by now that there *are* distinct differences in style between the major collections, as well as much continuity of theme and attitude. Poems in *The Whitsun Weddings*, for instance, show a more particular concern with the details of urban life than those in *The Less Deceived*, while in the second collection there are satirical poems like 'Naturally the Foundation will Bear Your Expenses', a type unrepresented in the first. Then, again in *High Windows*, such a poem as 'The Old Fools' deals with a familiar theme (age and death) but in a new way, so there are perceivable changes.

Did Larkin 'develop'?

The answer to this question could depend on how the word is defined: if 'developing' involves a revolution in thought and technique, it has to be 'no'. If it means the emergence of a new variety of subject and a greater accomplishment, the answer must be 'yes'. Yet Larkin did not think 'development' a helpful term, and you may well agree with him. Artists working in any medium are not all alike: some, like Keats, produce work which shows marked change during their creative lives. Others, like Larkin, don't change greatly and neither kind of artist is necessarily 'better' than the other. The question of 'development' is not, in fact, helpful in coming to an assessment of Larkin's achievement but it has to be considered, if for no other reason than that it figures so largely in criticism of his work during his life. In 1964 it clearly irritated him and he told Ian Hamilton:

> Oscar Wilde said that only mediocrities developed. I just don't know. I don't think I want to change; just to become better at what I am.[1]

By his fiftieth birthday in 1972, he had changed his mind a little and thought some differences might be desirable:

> What I should like to do is to write different kinds of poem that might be by different people. Someone said once that the great thing is not to be different from other people but to be different from yourself.[2]

Larkin chose 'The Explosion' from *High Windows* to illustrate this kind of difference but he could easily have chosen 'Livings' or 'Solar', for they too illustrate what was new in the last collection.

Larkin's stature – 'unofficial laureate'?

Critics have spilled much ink on forming a judgement on Larkin's stature as a writer and, indeed, that is the aim of this final chapter. I shall shortly be presenting you with different views of his work to consider and suggesting how you might come to an opinion of your own. Initially, you will have to be clear in your own mind as to what you mean by 'poetry' – not as a descriptive but as a *qualitative* term. The critic Colin Falck, for example, has definite, somewhat restrictive notions about its nature. For him, poetry should be concerned with acts of discrimination and discovering an order in life in terms of 'truth' and 'love', which are expressed in 'epiphanies', and these he finds lacking in Larkin's work:

> There are no epiphanies. Love and death, though they are the controlling ideas of the poems, can never inflame the individual moments of existence; instead they simply diminish them, and the boredom of this diminished existence is invested with a kind of absolute necessity. For, futile though life may be for the majority of people in our present society, it is not futile in principle in the way that Larkin makes it seem and by identifying himself with the drab, fantasy-haunted world of the waste land Larkin has not only downgraded the whole of real existence against an impossible absolute standard, but has also cut the ground from under the poet's feet.[3]

Consequently, for Falck, Larkin fails ultimately to *be* a poet, and, although these comments of his were made before the publication of *High Windows*, much of his argument could still stand, in spite of more affirmative poems in the collection like 'To the Sea' or 'Show Saturday'. It also has to be said that by Falck's definition a lot of what hitherto has been regarded as poetry would fall by the wayside.

How does a critic who is also a poet react to this kind of criticism? Donald Davie is also concerned with the world Larkin portrays but he is less prescriptive about what constitutes poetry. In a chapter of his book *Thomas Hardy and British Poetry*, he argues for a distinction between Larkin's 'philosophy' and the world of landscape and moods described in his poems, and so he does not discount Larkin's work on the grounds of the kind of beliefs he expresses. Davie is more interested in Larkin as a representative figure in post-war English poetry and believes that he is 'the central figure in English poetry over the last twenty years'. He also thought (in 1973) that 'there has been the widest possible agreement over most of this period, that Philip Larkin is for good or ill the effective unofficial laureate of post-1945 England',[4] because the observations in the poems of and on life (at least as regards *attitudes*) were wholly representative of many people's experience in the political and social world of post-war Britain. In that context, 'Larkin's poetry of lowered insights and patiently diminished expectations can be justified', though he went on to admit that 'he is so ready to lower his sights . . . that we begin to think he does so under pressure not from "the age" but only from some compulsion in himself'.[5]

For Davie, Larkin is the poet of and for a 'wholly urbanised and industrialised society'. As a spokesman for it, his work has a political dimension whether or not he is aware of it and, by implication, he settled for 'parliamentary democracy as a shabby, unavoidable best'.[6] Davie sees evidence for this in Larkin's 'perverse determination that the ultimate ('terminal') pastoral shall be among the cut-price stores, and nowhere else'[7], however patronising his attitude to the people who visit them might be. David sees this moderation as a welcome alternative to the politics of extreme Left or Right, the latter being tacitly fascist and associated with the Modernist movement which Larkin also rejected. It is an interesting argument and Larkin's representative quality is well described, but could not what Davie sees as *moderation* just as well be a degree of indifference? If anything, Larkin seems to have been more towards the 'Right' wing of politics, if we are to believe an interview in 1979 in which he claimed to 'adore Mrs Thatcher' at the beginning of her years as Prime Minister.[8]

'Provincialism'?

If Larkin was somewhat indifferent (or naïve?) about politics, it may be an illustration of another feature of his work which is often focused upon – his 'provincialism'. Charles Tomlinson, a poet whose view and practice of the art of poetry are quite disimilar to Larkin's, sees this as an intensely negative quality. Larkin's poems are 'often beautifully phrased', yet 'the possibilities of fulfilment seems almost wilfully short-circuited'.[9] Tomlinson's objections are most clearly expressed in an essay he wrote in 1959 – an essay which he has admitted he 'composed polemically from a standpoint that felt itself challenged by the publication, in 1955, of a number of verse manifestos, from the group known as the Movement'.[10] In his essay, he accused the writers in that group of 'self-congratulatory parochialism' and of lacking an interest in 'tradition' (by which he meant a European tradition).[11] Larkin and his fellows exhibited 'a provincial laziness of mind adopted as a public attitude and as the framework for an equally provincial verse'. In fact, as we now know, Larkin was much more aware of French poetry than he pretended to be. Nevertheless, is Tomlinson justified in seeing his work as narrow and circumscribed? And must 'provincial' always be a pejorative term, as it is for Tomlinson?

DISCUSSION

It is undeniable that Larkin's range is limited to subjects chosen from his own life and that which he observes around him, but this is quite deliberately done and is not a demonstration of inadequacy. For 'provincial' need not necessarily be used as a criticism. John Press uses it in his book *Rule and Energy* to describe, rather than to slight, Larkin, whereas Tomlinson he calls 'traditional'. The use of different terms is not intended to pass 'judgement on their respective merits' but is an attempt 'to indicate the distinctive cast of their minds and the nature of their aesthetic principles'.[12] To Press, 'provincial' is not a disparaging term but describes a poet

> ... who is primarily concerned with the values of his own cultural society, and who is largely indifferent to what lies beyond the world that he knows at first hand. Thus he cares very little for the poetry and the civilisation of other ages and other countries, nor does he feel

the need to justify his own practice by reference to the past. He values above all else sincerity of feeling, fidelity to the truth as he conceives it.[13]

No doubt Press had Larkin in mind when he formulated this definition, for the description fits most of his work closely. It is not, however, purely a descriptive term since Press ends his survey of poems from *The Less Deceived* by raising a common question whereby 'provincial' takes on a distinctly unflattering meaning: by 'confining himself to a closed circle of emotions, and to a limited intellectual range', has Larkin 'stunted the growth of his inner life and of his art, condemning himself to a self-inflicted provincialism of the mind and of the sensibility'?[14]. Without actually agreeing with this view, Press (who is clearly of the 'Growth is development' school of critics) cautiously concludes that Larkin may prove 'one of those very good (but not major) poets whose art steadily becomes more exact, discriminating, and assured without undergoing any radical transformation or development'.[15] Leaving aside for the moment whether or not Larkin is 'major', this proved to be an accurate prediction.

'Symbolist' elements?

On the whole, Press is right when he suggests that Larkin's work shows little interest in 'the civilisation of other ages and other countries', but this is clearly by choice rather than ignorance, for he demonstrably has an interest, however peripheral, in French poetry. Andrew Motion has convincingly shown how one of Larkin's earliest published poems, 'Femmes Damnées' (written in 1943) strongly echoes Baudelaire's poem of the same title, and he goes on to quote Larkin's own comment on his poem 'Absences' (*The Less Deceived*, p. 40):

> I fancy it sounds like a different, better poet than myself. The last line sounds like a slightly unconvincing translation from a French symbolist. I wish I could write like this more often.[16]

He was speaking of these lines:

> Above the sea, the yet more shoreless day,
> Riddled by wind, trails lit-up galleries:
> they shift to giant ribbing, sift away.
> Such attics cleared of me! Such absences!

As Motion points out, the final line 'appropriately, includes the poem's most radical, imaginative jump – from sea to attics and from attics to absence itself'.[17] Writing in this style is aptly described as 'symbolist' even if it occurs only occasionally, for ideas and feelings are conveyed obliquely, impersonally and complexly (though perhaps obscurely).

A 'modernist' inheritance?

In drawing attention to the appropriateness of the 'leap' to the poem's final line, Andrew Motion raises the issue of 'expressive form' – that is, how the shape and arrangement of the poem can contribute to its substance. The critic Simon Petch sees Larkin's concern with this aspect of writing as one characteristic he shares with the 'modernist' artists he claims to dislike:

> Larkin never forgets that the act of reading a poem is itself part of that poem's action, and thus the complexity of a poem's coherence on the page is frequently used to stimulate our perception of the poem's thematic meaning. . . . He has become adept at exploiting such things as typographical variation, the fact that rhymes are sometimes seen rather than heard, and the visual organisation of line-ending and stanza-arrangement. Such technical features may function in a poem as mimetic puns or enactments of its statement . . . It would be misleading to suggest that these things are peculiar to modernism, but the visual organisation of a written work of art as an essential aspect of its total meaning has been fiercely adopted by modernist writers. . . .[18]

It is undoubtedly true that Larkin's work does show these admirable features, but they are certainly not 'peculiar to modernism' – they can be found in the poems of George Herbert (1593–1633) or, indeed, Hardy. And the same qualification can be added to Petch's observation that Larkin's use of different 'speakers' or *personae* in poems like 'Vers de Société' or 'Posterity' (*High Windows*, p. 35, p. 27) is a version of modernist 'masks', to use Pound's terms. And it has to be said that *most* of Larkin's poems do not work in this fashion. In my view, Petch is more convincing when he points out the 'dangers' as he sees them of Larkin trying to write 'like a symbolist' – that is, in a poem like 'Absences' (quoted above) the risk of obscurity. And I think he is right when he claims that Larkin's more successful writing in this style is to be found in *The Whitsun Weddings* where there are 'fewer imaginary symbols, such as the ships of 'Next, Please', and more familiar, naturalistic ones'.[19] But do these 'symbolist' and 'modernist' elements really amount not much? In my opinion, they are only peripheral to the main body of the verse, though they do show that there has always been a greater range of style and a larger debt to the past than has sometimes been acknowledged.

The major theme

Through his four collections, Larkin's choice of subject did become more varied, but not greatly so, and there was no change in the fundamental outlook which so strongly informs the three major volumes. The explicit statements about life's lack of direction remained substantially the same and there was no attempt to explain events in political or religious terms. Indeed, if anything, the dismissal of religion in particular became more explicit as the obsession with death became stronger, though this was not at the expense of the conviction that nevertheless life was well worth living. 'Aubade', Larkin's last major poem published in *The Times Literary Supplement* in December 1977 shows his continuing preoccupation with human mortality very clearly, and six years later he was still writing about it when reviewing *The Oxford Book of Death*. It was his opinion that 'the majority view . . . [is that] . . . death is the end of everything', and, reflecting almost hopefully on the book's slim chance of commercial success, he concludes:

> If so, serve them right. For in the last analysis the intrusion of death into our lives is so ruthless, so irreversible, so rarely unaccompanied by pain, terror and remorse, that to 'anthologise' it, however calmly, quizzically and compassionately, seems at best irrelevant, at worst an error of taste.[20]

Death was the subject Larkin wrote about continually and powerfully, with imagination and a strong sense of its imminence and inevitability. It was an aspect of life that he could never, in any way, come to terms with. There was, for him, no religious explanation or reassurance, and neither could he find solace in existentialist, stoicist or whatever other kind of belief. In that sense, he was indeed a very earthbound poet for whom reality was the world within his view or within his memory.

This quality is also evident in the other main theme in Larkin's work, one related to death – the dimension of time within which we live. As Donald Davie has pointed out, Larkin is like Hardy in his mistrust of 'the claims of poetry to transcend the linear unrolling of time', in contrast to Yeats who 'exerts himself repeatedly to transcend historical time by seeing it as cyclical, so as to leap above it into a realm that is visionary, mythological, and (in some sense or some degree) *eternal*'. In this sense, Larkin's 'conversion' from

Yeats to Hardy after *The North Ship* had an 'emblematic significance'.[21] Like Hardy, Larkin often reflects (usually sadly) on the passage of time but he does not see it in terms of metaphysics. Rather, it is something of a puzzle to him:

> What are days for?
> Days are where we live.
>
> ('Days', *The Whitsun Weddings*, p. 27)

And time is menacing because the realisation that things have changed irrevocably is an indication of a kind of erosion:

> Truly, though our element is time,
> We are not suited to the long perspectives
> Open at each instant of our lives.
> they link us to our losses . . .
>
> ('Reference Back', *The Whitsun Weddings*, p. 40)

Larkin sees human life caught in an irresolvable paradox – we are creatures of time, yet that fact does not suit us. That he does not, or cannot, resolve this intellectually is because it is a metaphysical question. Whether he had any definable 'philosophy' is open to doubt and in a sense his thinking had a very 'English' cast to it in that he seemed uninterested in, perhaps mistrustful of, ideas – ideas as being interesting in themselves or as part of a wider scheme of thought whether religious, philosophical, political or whatever. It is for this reason that his verse could not properly be described as metaphysical, in spite of the paradoxical nature of some of his conclusions. Larkin's paradoxes cannot be rendered acceptable as those of, say, John Donne can. The final lines of Donne's 'Holy Sonnets: X' illustrate this:

> One short sleepe past, wee wake eternally,
> And death shall be no more; death thou shalt die.

Time and death – these are Larkin's themes too but he relates them only to specific situations and is not interested in developing them through argument or exposition. These ideas are therefore limited for him and become a self-imposed, restricting factor in the poetry. This is the fundamental nature of the verse Larkin writes. Is it a flaw, or a source of stoical strength?

DISCUSSION

You might argue that you can't criticise a poet for the poems he has *not* written, and Larkin said more than once that his purpose in writing was to record individual experiences and feelings rather than to depict the grand order of things. On the other hand, these

experiences frequently involve 'death', 'life', 'love', 'time', all
themes which have long been recognised as the subjects of serious
art and which certainly invite interpretation in terms of *some* kind
of philosophy. Anthony Thwaite has argued that the very existence
of such 'unshakeably major themes' combined with an 'authentic
gravity' is an indication of the importance of Larkin's work.[22]

But is this in itself enough? Does the mere presence of what
are, after all, quite common ideas in art indicate stature? Does not
the degree of achievement depend on depth of response and the
quality of reflection on them? David Timms, a sympathetic
commentator on Larkin's work, has argued eloquently that his
treatment of suffering and disappointment (which figure largely in
the poems) can actually be seen as 'positive' because, by recognising
and facing up to them, the speaker suffers a 'maturing' experience.
He thinks Larkin resembles Hardy in this respect and, in support of
his argument, he quotes from a review by Larkin of a book on
Hardy in which 'suffering or sadness' is described as 'an intensely
maturing experience'.[23] In the same review, Larkin goes on to point
out how Hardy thought that suffering in life was 'true' and that
sensitivity to it was associated with 'superior spiritual character'.
He concluded

> ... that the presence of pain in Hardy's novels is a positive, not a
> negative, quality – not the mechanical working out of some
> pre-determined allegiance to pessimism or any other concept, but the
> continual imaginative celebration of what is both the truest and the
> most important element in life, most important in the sense of most
> necessary to spiritual development.[24]

This is a good argument, but it can't really be used accurately
with respect to Larkin's own work, in which there is little evidence
of 'spiritual development' in the way that there is in, say, a novel
like *Tess of the d'Urbervilles*, though there is plenty of what Larkin
calls the 'melancholy, the misfortunate, the frustrating, the failing
elements of life'.[25] It isn't that Larkin lacks sensitivity to, or is
unaware of, these things, but he does not achieve any kind of
resolution and his basic response does not develop. It is, essentially,
an attitude of passivity, as he explained to his first publisher in
1955:

> ... my fundamentally passive attitude to poetry (and life too, I
> suppose) ... believes that the agent is always more deceived than the
> patient, because action comes from desire, and we all know that
> desire comes from wanting something we haven't got, which may
> not make us any happier when we have it. On the other hand
> suffering – well, there is positively no deception about that. No one
> *imagines* their suffering.[26]

Your first reaction to the last remark might well be that plenty of people do imagine or magnify their 'suffering', but the general point is clear – only a masochist would actually seek it out.

Autobiography?

Larkin's concentration on the frustrations of life raises another question – is the range of feelings and attitudes in the poetry that of the poet himself? (In other words, the 'biographical question' again.) To some extent it has to be, but as Larkin pointed out to Ian Hamilton, 'poems are artificial in the sense that a play is artificial'.[27] Like parts in a play, the poem is often written through a *persona* or *personae* which may or may not be fairly close to the author but which will, in any case, be modulated or intensified for greater effect. But it is unlikely that the poet is *always* ventriloquising, and one way of deciding whether he is speaking *in propria persona* is by judging the tone of the discourse. Thus, you might be tempted to say that the narrator of 'The Whitsun Weddings' is probably the 'poet himself' because the tone is uncomplicated, straightforward, and also because you might reasonably infer that he is, like Larkin, an artist and a bachelor.

In fact, Larkin admitted on several occasions that his work *was* very autobiographical. (Indeed, he had qualms about publishing *The Less Deceived* just before moving to the public position of Librarian at the University of Hull because, as he told George Hartley, 'my poems are nothing if not personal'.)[28] In all probability, many of the attitudes expressed were Larkin's own. On the other hand, what help, if any, is this when reading the poems? Larkin, although a private man, made himself accessible by giving interviews but they don't help very much in talking about the poetry. Indeed, the more puristically minded who see texts as distinct and inviolable might argue that biographical information could distort and obscure possible readings, and render subtleties imperceptible. This is not to say (though some would) that every text, every poem in this case, is *completely* 'open' to any reading a person cares to make a case for. What it does mean is that an excessive identification between Larkin and the poems could, for example, make a feminist perspective on his work more difficult than it need be. (Larkin, after all, gives the impression of being likeable and sympathetic as a man; that is not to say that a feminist critic would take kindly to his work, and so identifying the two is confusing.) The more scrupulously minded might wish to argue that biography is *never* relevant and always distorting, and the case

can be made. With Larkin, however, who was (whether he liked it
or not) a public figure, knowledge about him is almost inescapable
(cherished by some, it could be said). All the more reason, then, to
be aware of the problems such information can cause in
interpreting the poetry. But what matters in the end in the poetry
which is more or less autobiographical is that the personal
experience is so elaborated as to be no longer singular but general,
so that readers can 'find' their own lives in it.

Wounded art?

One quality which did emerge in interviews and which is certainly
present in the poetry was his fundamental pessimism and it raises
the question whether the poetry *qua* poetry is wounded by this.
Colin Falck, with his particular emphasis on the need for
'epiphanies', thought that it was. For Clive James, on the other
hand, the very strength of the verse lies in its limitations: the 'poetic
intensity', he argues, is directly related to the 'circumscription of
Larkin's view of life' and it is wrong to assume that 'just because
the poet is (self-admittedly) emotionally wounded, the poetry is
wounded too'. In his view, though 'it ought to be obvious that
Larkin is not a universal poet in the thematic sense (because he is a
'self-proclaimed stranger to a good half, *the* good half of life'),
nevertheless 'the poetry is all there'.[29] James thus accepts what
Falck cannot and believes that there is 'consensus about his stature'
in the sense that, subjects apart, he was a poet of exceptional skill
who wrote verse of a striking and original kind. In my view, he is
correct, and future generations reading poetry written in English
will judge his work as a major achievement.

A 'great' poet?

Is Larkin a 'great' poet? For Colin Falck, certainly not, because of
the *kind* of poetry he writes; and his is a moral judgement, whereas
Clive James concerns himself with literary matters only. Should one
apply moral or philosophical standards to judgements of this kind?
Would a feminist critic, for example, be 'wrong' to see 'Sunny
Prestatyn' quite differently from my reading (see p. 57)? S/he might
argue that the poem demonstrates the exploitation of women in a
patriarchal society, women (in the figure of the model) being
subjected to 'male violence' in the despoliation of the poster.
(Could it be said that such a reading is 'wrong', even if the author

himself had denied it? Or does it tell you more about the critic than the poem?) Would someone with religious beliefs feel compelled to deny Larkin major status because, although he claimed to be seeking truth, he describes their outlook as superstitious? The poet and critic T. S. Eliot would have felt this because he believed that

> literary criticism should be completed by criticism from a definite ethical and theological standpoint and that the greatness of literature cannot be determined solely by literary standards; though whether it is literature or not can be determined only by literary standards.[30]

In general, it is a point of view I share but somehow it is a measure that does not seem especially applicable to Larkin. The issue would loom larger had he been a didactic poet (like Hugh MacDiarmid, or Eliot himself in later years) but Larkin was not a systematic moralist. His aim was to record his own experiences honestly in a manner calculated to give pleasure. As he told John Haffenden, one of the mistakes made about him was to assume that he was a 'protest poet' (even of as mild a kind as Betjeman might be said to be).[31] He did not seek to 'convert' the reader to his point of view, though he certainly had one. How does Larkin fare by 'literary standards', as Eliot calls them? If you were asked to describe his poems to someone, what would you say?

DISCUSSION & CONCLUSION

I think I would find myself saying that he shows several kinds of paradox as a poet: he was not an innovator in his use of language in the way that, say, James Joyce was, yet he did add to the English language by his coining of phrases like 'lucent comb' ('The Building') which echo in the mind long after the poem has been put aside. He is generally an accessible poet but not thereby a simple one (the thought is often sophisticated), yet sometimes he can be obscure. Allied to this is his frequent use of colloquial language, yet this is masterfully dove-tailed with the long cadence. I think I might also want to convey something of the tone of the poems – compassionate, witty, and, above all, really rather sad, often like the jazz blues he was so fond of.[32] It is a unique intonation and one that before his death had come to be known as 'Larkinesque'. It is a safe bet that the word will continue to be used and that in itself is testimony to his achievement.

Notes

Chapter 1: Larkin's Life and Career (Pages 1–8)

1 'An Interview with the *Observer*', 16 December 1979, *Required Writing*, Faber 1983, p. 48.
2 'The South Bank Show', 30 May 1982, London Weekend Television.
3 Noel Hughes, 'The Young Mr Larkin', in Anthony Thwaite (ed.), *Larkin At Sixty*, Faber, 1982, pp. 24–5.
4 'A Voice For Our Time', *Required Writing*, pp. 48–9.
5 David Timms, *Philip Larkin*, Oliver & Boyd, 1978, p. 4.
6 'An Interview with the *Observer*', *Required Writing*, Faber, 1983, pp. 48–9.
7 See Kingsley Amis. 'Oxford and After', in Anthony Thwaite (ed.), *Larkin At Sixty*, Faber, 1982, pp. 24–5.
8 *Ibid.*, p. 27.
9 'The South Bank Show', 30 May 1982, London Weekend Television.
10 Timms, *op. cit.*, p. 7.
11 *Required Writing*, Faber, 1982, p. 34.
12 Interviewed by A. N. Wilson, BBC Radio 4, 29 March 1984.
13 'Something to be Said', BBC Radio 3, 29 May 1986 (repeat from February 1986).
14 *op. cit.*, p. 28.
15 Radio 4 Interview, 29 March 1984.
16 'The South Bank Show', 30 May 1982, London Weekend Television.
17 'An Interview with the *Observer*', *Required Writing*, Faber, 1983, p. 51.
18 Radio 4 Interview, 29 March 1984.
19 Radio 4 Interview, 29 March 1984.
20 For a discussion of this point, see Timms, *op. cit., p. 9.*
21 Charles Monteith, 'Publishing Larkin', in Anthony Thwaite (ed), *Larkin At Sixty*, Faber, 1982, p. 42.
22 Monteith, *op. cit.*, p. 45.
23 John Osbourne, 'Philip Larkin', *Lincolnshire & Humberside Arts Diary*, March–April 1986, p. 7.
24 'Philip Larkin 1922–1985', BBC 2 TV, 1 January 1986.
25 'An Interview with the *Paris Review*', *Paris Review*, No. 84, 1982, p. 72.
26 BBC Radio 4, 29 March 1984.

27   'The South Bank Show', 30 May 1982, London Weekend Television.
28   Radio 4 Interview, 29 March 1984.
29   BBC TV, *Monitor*, 1964.
30   'An Interview with the *Observer*'. Faber, 1983, p. 54.
31   *The Times*, 14 December 1985, p. 10.
32   BBC Radio 4, 29 March 1984.
33   *Ibid.*
34   Douglas Dunn, 'Memoirs of the Brynmor Jones Library', in Anthony
     Thwaite (ed.), *Larkin At Sixty*, Faber, 1982, p. 54.
35   'An Interview with the *Observer*', Faber, 1983, p. 54.
36   *Ibid.*
37   *Ibid.*
38   Amis, *op. cit.*, p. 30.
39   Amis, *op. cit.*, p. 29.
40   George Hartley, 'Nothing to be Said', in Anthony Thwaite (ed.),
     Larkin At Sixty, Faber, 1982, p. 89.
41   'On the Plain of Holderness', in Anthony Thwaite (ed.), *Larkin At
     Sixty*, Faber, 1982, p. 68.

Chapter 2: What Kind of Poet is Larkin? (Pages 9–15)

1   'An Interview with the Paris Review', *Paris Review*, No. 84, 1982,
    p. 62.
2   Anon., 'Speaking of Writing XIII: Philip Larkin.' From Our Special
    Correspondent, *The Times*, 20 February 1964, p. 16.
3   *Times Literary Supplement*, 23 December 1977, p. 1491.
4   *Required Writing*, Faber, 1982, p. 54.
5   'White' is a slang word used in Larkin's novel *Jill* to mean 'decent'.
6   'An Interview with the *Paris Review*', *Paris Review*, No. 84, 1982,
    p. 68.

Chapter 3: Novelist into Poet (Pages 15–34)

1   Ian Hamilton, 'Four Conversations', *London Magazine*, Vol. IV,
    No. 6, November 1964, p. 75.
2   *Philip Larkin*, (Contemporary Writers Series), Methuen, 1982, p. 48.
3   *Op. cit.*, p. 55.
4   Barbara Pym, *A Very Private Eye*, Hilary Pym and Hazel Holt, (eds),
    Macmillan, 1984, p. 226. Letter dated 7 April 1964.
5   *Required Writing*, Faber, 1983, pp. 95–6.
6   *Ibid.*, p. 94.
7   'Philip Massinger', *Selected Essays*, Faber 1932, p. 206.
8   Timms, *op. cit.*, p. 55.
9   *Collected Shorter Poems 1927–1957*, Faber, 1969, p. 13.
10 'Something to be Said', BBC Radio 3, 29 May 1986 (repeated from
    February 1986).
11 'Philip Larkin Praises the Poetry of Thomas Hardy', reprinted in *The
    Listener*, 25 July 1968, p. 111.
12 *Times Educational Supplement*, 13 July 1956, p. 933.
13 'The Blending of Betjeman', *The Spectator*, 2 December 1960, p. 913.
14 'Betjeman en Bloc', *Listen*, III, No. 2, Spring 1959.

15 Ian Hamilton, 'Four Conversations', *London Magazine*, Vol. IV, No. 6, November 1964, pp. 71–2.
16 *The Spectator*, 2 December 1960, p. 913.
17 'Speaking of Writing XIII: Philip Larkin', *The Times*, 20 February 1964, p. 16.
18 'The Pleasure Principle', *Listen*, II, No. 3, Summer–Autumn 1957, p. 30.
19 'The Pleasure Principle', p. 28.
20 Ian Hamilton, 'Four Conversations', *London Magazine*, Vol. IV, No. 6, November 1964, p. 71.
21 *The Movement*, Oxford University Press, 1980, p. 9.
22 Ian Hamilton, 'Four Conversations', p. 72.

Chapter 4: *The Less Deceived* (Page 34–46)

1 A title Larkin found satisfactorily 'neutral'.
2 *Op. cit.*, p. 75.
3 *Op. cit.*, p. 86.
4 Ian Hamilton, 'Four Conversations', *London Magazine*, Vol. IV, No. 6, November 1964, p. 75.
5 The sentiment is familiar. 'I Remember, I Remember' develops the theme, using speech to dramatise a narrative account.
6 'The Poet Speaks', PLP 1088, Record Eight (Argo Record Company).
7 Ian Hamilton, 'Four Conversations', p. 73.
8 John Haffenden, *Viewpoints. Poets in Conversations*. Faber, 1981, p. 124.
9 Ian Hamilton, 'Four Conversations', p. 74.
10 And there is every reason to suppose that it is since the poem is clearly autobiographical – Larkin admitted this to Sir John Betjeman in the BBC 'Monitor' interview (1964).

Chapter 5: *The Whitsun Weddings* (Pages 47–63)

1 'Philip Larkin', *Encounter*, XIII, May 1964, p. 72.
2 Ian Hamilton, 'Four Conversations', *London Magazine*, Vol. IV, No. 6, November 1964, p. 76.
3 'Philip Larkin', in Ian Hamilton (ed.), *The Modern Poet: Essays from 'The Review'*, Macdonald, 1968, p. 110.
4 *The London Magazine*, Vol. 4, No. 2, May 1964, p. 73.
5 Ian Hamilton, 'Four Conversations', p. 76.
6 Marvell Press, LPV6 (Cassette: Marvell Press *Listen* Cassettes).
7 *Philip Larkin*, Oliver and Boyd, 1973, p. 95. It is evident, too, in other poems e.g. 'The Large Cool Store', p. 30.
8 'Engagement or Withdrawal: Some Notes on the Work of Philip Larkin', *Critical Quarterly*, Vol. VI, Summer 1964, pp. 174–5.
9 Anthony Thwaite, 'The Poetry of Philip Larkin', *Phoenix*, Nos. 11/12, Autumn and Winter, 1973–4, p. 51.
10 'The South Bank Show', 30 May 1982, London Weekend Television.
11 *Ibid.*
12 *Ibid.*
13 Ian Hamilton, 'Four Conversations', p. 74.

14   'Philip Larkin reads *The Whitsun Weddings*', Marvell Press LPV6.
15   *Ibid.*
16   *Ibid.*

Chapter 6: *High Windows* and After (Pages 63–81)

1   Ian Hamilton, 'Four Conversations', *London Magazine*, Vol. IV,
     No. 6, November 1964, p. 75.
2   Vol. 73, No. 4, January 1984, p. 4.
3   Reprinted in the *Observer*, 29 December 1985. It was one of a collec-
     tion put together secretly by the poet's wife.
4   The offer came in a hand-written letter from the Prime Minister when
     the death of Sir John Betjeman left the post vacant, according to
     'Justin Browser', 'Diary' in *The Literary Review*, January 1986, p. 3.
     According to Kingsley Amis, one of the reasons Larkin refused it was
     because of the publicity it would have brought him.
5   'Betjeman en Bloc', *Listen*, Vol. III, No. 2, Spring 1959, p. 19.
6   'Philip Larkin', *The Spectator*, 7 December 1985, p. 24.
7   'An Interview with the *Observer*', *Required Writing*, Faber, 1983,
     p. 55.
8   *A New Translation*, Collins Fontana, 1966, p. 179.
9   John Haffenden, *Viewpoints: Poets in Conversation*, Faber, 1981,
     p. 128.
10   *Ibid.*, p. 127.
11   *Ibid.*, p. 128.
12   *Ibid.*, p. 127.
13   *Ibid.*, p. 127.
14   Psalm 72, *A New Translation*, Collins Fontana, 1966, p. 127.
15   'Philip Larkin: After Symbolism', *Essays in Criticism*, Vol. XXX,
     No. 3, July 1980, p. 237.
16   John Haffenden, *op. cit.*, p. 124.
17   Ian Hamilton, 'Four Conversations', p. 77.
18   Clive James, 'Wolves of Memory', *Encounter*, June 1974, p. 65.
19   Haffenden, *op. cit.*, p. 127–8.

Chapter 7: Larkin's Achievement (Pages 82–93)

1   Ian Hamilton, 'Four Conversations', *London Magazine*, Vol. IV,
     No. 6, November 1964, p. 77.
2   'Out of the Air: Not like Larkin', *The Listener*, 17 August 1972,
     p. 209.
3   'Philip Larkin', in Ian Hamilton (ed.), *The Modern Poet: Essays From
     'The Review'*, Macdonald, 1968, p. 00.
4   *Thomas Hardy and British Poetry*, Routledge & Kegan Paul, 1972,
     p. 64.
5   *Ibid.*, p. 71, p. 80.
6   *Ibid.*, p. 74.
7   *Ibid.*, p. 81.
8   'An Interview with the *Observer*', *Required Writing*, Faber, 1983,
     p. 52.

9 'Some Aspects of Poetry Since the War', in Boris Ford (ed.), *The New Pelican Guide to English Literature*, Vol. 8, *The Present*, Penguin, 1983, p. 457.

10 *Ibid.*, p. 450.

11 'Poetry Today', in Boris Ford (ed.), *The Pelican Guide to English Literature*, Vol. 7, *The Modern Age*, Penguin, 1964, p. 458.

12 *Rule and Energy*, Oxford University Press, 1963, p. 90.

13 *Ibid.*, p. 91.

14 *Ibid.*, p. 91.

15 *Ibid.*, p. 105.

16 Paul Engle and Joseph Langland (eds), *Poet's Choice*, New York, Dial Press, 1962, p. 202. Quoted in Andrew Motion, *Philip Larkin*, Methuen, 1982, p. 74.

17 *Ibid.*, p. 75.

18 *The Art of Philip Larkin*, Sydney University Press, 1981, p. 8.

19 *Ibid.*, p. 70.

20 'Point of No Return', the *Observer*, 24 April 1983, p. 30.

21 *Thomas Hardy and British Poetry*, Routledge & Kegan Paul, 1973, p. 4.

22 'The Poetry of Philip Larkin', *Phoenix*, 11/12 Autumn/Winter 1973–4, p. 57.

23 *Philip Larkin*, Oliver & Boyd, 1973, pp. 58–9.

24 'Wanted: Good Hardy Critic', *Critical Quarterly*, VIII, Summer 1966, pp. 177–8.

25 *Ibid.*, p. 177.

26 George Hartley, 'Nothing to be Said', in Anthony Thwaite (ed.), *Larkin At Sixty*, Faber, 1982, p. 88.

27 'Four Conversations', *London Magazine*, London VI, 6 November 1964, p. 74.

28 George Hartley, 'Nothing to be Said', in Anthony Thwaite (ed.), *Larkin At Sixty*, Faber, 1982.

29 'Wolves of Memory', *Encounter*, Vol. XLII, No. 6, June 1974, p. 66.

30 'Religion and Literature', in John Hayward (ed.), *Selected Prose*, Penguin Books, 1953, p. 31.

31 *Op. cit.*, p. 119.

32 Alistair Cook pointed out in a programme made for, and dedicated to, the memory of Larkin that the classic 'blues' number was usually a sad song by an individual ('Nothing But the Blues', BBC Radio 4, 25 June 1986). The parallel with Larkin's lyrics hardly needs pointing out.

Further Reading and a Select Bibliography

In view of Larkin's death in 1985, the next few years will probably see the publication of a number of items about him. The official biography is being written by his friend and literary executor, Andrew Motion. Though all of Larkin's private diaries were destroyed after his death in accordance with his wishes, there are a number of unpublished items which may well be preserved for posterity.

The suggestions that follow are a selection only of the many articles and publications which have appeared in Larkin's work over the last thirty years. The standard bibliography is *Philip Larkin: A Bibliography 1933–76* by B.C. Bloomfield, Faber, 1979.

Works in Prose and Verse by Philip Larkin

LARKIN, PHILIP ARTHUR

- (1945) *The North Ship*, Fortune Press. Second Edition, introduced by Philip Larkin, and has an additional poem taken from *XX Poems*, Faber, 1966.
- (1946) *Jill*, Fortune Press. Second edition introduced by Philip Larkin, Faber, 1964.
- (1947) *A Girl in Winter*, Faber.
- (1951) *XX Poems*. Privately printed in limited edition – 100 copies. Belfast.
- (1954) *Fantasy Press: Pamphlet No. 21*, Swineford.
- (1955) *The Less Deceived* , Hessle, Marvell Press.
- (1964) *The Whitsun Weddings*, Faber.
- (1974) *High Windows*, Faber.

(1970)   *All What Jazz: A Record Diary 1961–68*, Faber.
(1978)   Femes Damnées. Sycamore Broadsheet No. 27, Oxford,
         Sycamore Press.
(1983)   *Required Writing. Miscellaneous Pieces 1955–1982*,
         Faber.
LARKIN, PHILIP ARTHUR(ed.)
(1973)   *The Oxford Book of Twentieth-Century Verse*. Oxford,
         Clarendon Press.

Manuscripts

At present, the only manuscripts in public collections are:
Jill, the printer's copy for the second, Faber edition which Larkin
gave to the Bodleian Library, Oxford in 1965.
Manuscript Notebook (October 1944 to March 1950), containing
autograph drafts, revisions etc. Presented to the British Library
Department of Manuscripts for the Arts Council Collection of
Modern Literary Manuscripts.

Special Collection

The Brynmor Jones Library at the University of Hull where Larkin
was Librarian for the last thirty years of his life has a special Philip
Larkin Collection. There is no manuscript material apart from
letter to Harry Chambers, the publisher of *Phoenix* Magazine, but
there are first editions, translations of Larkin's work and a valuable
assortment of audio-visual items, recordings, interviews etc. with
him.

Uncollected Poems

'Tops', *Listen*, II, Spring 1957, p. 6.
'Success Story', *Beloit Poetry Journal*, No. III, No. 4, Winter 1961,
    p. 309.
'Breadfruit', *Critical Quarterly*, Vol. III, No. 4, Winter 1961,
    p. 309.
'Love', *Critical Quarterly*, VIII, Summer 1966, p. 173.
'How Distant', *The Listener*, 28 October 1967, p. 521.
'A Couplet by Philip Larkin', *Black Paper II: the Crisis in
    Education*, C. B. Cox and A. E. Dyson (eds), 1969, p. 133.
'Heads in the Woman's Ward', *New Humanist*, I, May 1972, p. 17.
'Continuing to Live', in *A Keepsake from the New Library*, School
    of Oriental and African Studies, University of London, 1973,
    p. 9.

'The Life with a Hole in It', *Poetry Supplement*, Poetry Book Society, 1974, reprinted in *New Poems 1975: A PEN Anthology of Contemporary Poetry*, Hutchinson, 1975, p. 97.
'Aubade', *Times Literary Supplement*, 23 December 1977, p. 1491. Reprinted in *Poetry Book Society Anthology 1986–7*, J. Barker (ed.), 1986, p. 64.
'Party Politics', *Poetry Review*, Vol. 73, No.4, January 19894, p. 4.
'Modesties', *Poetry Book Society Anthology 1986–7*, J. Barker, (ed.), 1986, p. 61.
'Success Story', *Poetry Book Society Anthology 1986–7*, J. Barker (ed.), 1986, p. 62.
'How', *Poetry Book Society Anthology 1986–7*, J. Barker (ed.), 1986, p. 63.

A Selection of Uncollected Essays and Reviews by Larkin
'Betjeman en Bloc', *Listen*, III, Spring, 1959, pp. 14–22.
'Context: Philip Larkin', *London Magazine*, I, February, 1962, pp. 31–2. [Larkin on writing and experience.]
'Philip Larkin Praises the Poetry of Thomas Hardy', *The Listener*, 25 July 1968, p. 111. [An extract from a radio programme in which Larkin had explained the importance of Hardy to him.]
'Stevie, Good-bye', *The Observer*, 23 January 1972, p. 28 [Written after Stevie Smith's death.]
'The State of Poetry – A Symposium: Philip Larkin', *The Review*, 29–30, Spring–Summer 1972, p. 60.
'Amis and Auden', *The New Review*, Vol. 5, No. 2, 1978, pp. 92–4.
'Things Noticed', *New Statesman*, 4 May 1979, pp. 642–3. [Reviews the personal notebooks of Hardy.]
'Horror Poet', *Poetry Review*, Vol. 72, No. 1, pp. 51–3. [Review of Sylvia Plath's *Collected Poems*.]
'Point of No Return', *The Observer*, 24 April 1983, p. 30. [Review of *The Oxford Book of Death*.]

Selected Criticism

Books

TIMMS, DAVID, *Philip Larkin*, Oliver & Boyd, 1973). [The first study of Larkin's work and therefore somewhat out of date, but still a useful introduction to the earlier period which pays close, sympathetic attention to the novels and poetry.]
BROWNJOHN, ALAN, *Philip Larkin*. No. 247 in the Writers and their Work series, Longman for the British Council, 1975.

PETCH, SIMON, *The Art of Philip Larkin*, Sydney University Press, 1981. [A general introduction with useful discussion of particular poems, including those from *High Windows* which Timms does not cover.]

MOTION, ANDREW, *Philip Larkin*, Methuen, 1982. [A stimulating discussion of both novels and poems which argues that the 'Symbolist mode associated with Yeats' is more important in Larkin's work than is usually recognised'. Assumes familiarity with Larkin's work.]

WHALEN, TERRY, *Philip Larkin and English Poetry*, Macmillan, 1986.

Articles

Phoenix, 'Philip Larkin Issue', Nos. 11/12, Autumn and Winter 1973–4. [A most useful collection, containing fourteen essays and the worksheets of 'At Grass'.]

Bateson, F. W., 'Auden's (and Empson's) Heirs', *Essays in Criticism*, VII, January 1957, pp. 76–80. [In part a review of The Less Deceived.]

Bayley, John, 'Too good for this world', *Times Literary Supplement*, 21 June 1974, pp. 653–5. [Review of *High Windows*.]

Betjeman, John, 'Common Experiences', *The Listener*, 19 March 1964, p. 483.

Brownjohn, Alan, 'The Deep Blue Air', *New Statesman*, 14 June 1974, pp. 854–6. [Review of *High Windows*.]

Chambers, Harry, 'The Poetry of Philip Larkin', *Phoenix*, 9, Summer 1963, pp. 30–36.

Cox, C. B., 'Philip Larkin', *Critical Quarterly*, I, Spring 1959, pp. 14–17. [Analyses poems from *The Less Deceived*.]

Dodsworth, Martin, 'The Climate of Pain in Recent Poetry', *London Magazine*, IV, November 1964, pp. 86–95.

Falck, Colin, 'Philip Larkin', in Hamilton, Ian (ed.), *The Modern Poet: Essays from 'The Review'*, Macdonald, 1968.

Ferguson, Peter, 'Philip Larkin's *XX Poems*: The Missing Link', *Agenda*, Vol. 14, No. 3, Autumn 1976, pp. 53–65. [Examines in some detail the seven poems not subsequently published in *The Less Deceived*.]

Gardner, Philip, 'Bearing the Unbearable', *Phoenix*, No. 13, Spring 1975, p. 94. [Review of *High Windows*.]

Gardner, Philip, 'The Wintry Drum: The Poetry of Philip Larkin', *Dalhousie Reviews*, XLVIII, Spring 1968, pp. 88–99.

Hamilton, Ian, 'The Whitsun Weddings', *London Magazine*, IV, May 1964, pp. 70–74.

Hamilton, Ian, 'The Making of the Movement', *New Statesman*, 23 April 1971.

Hartley, George, 'The Lost Displays', *Phoenix*, No. 13, Spring 1975, p. 94. Review of *High Windows*.

James, Clive, 'Wolves of Memory', *Encounter*, June 1974, pp. 65–71. Review of *High Windows*.

Swinden, Patrick, 'Old Lines, New Lines: The Movement Ten Years After', *Critical Quarterly*, IX, Winter 1967, pp. 347–59. Contains interesting comparison of Larkin with Thom Gunn.

Thwaite, Anthony, 'The Poetry of Philip Larkin', in Dodsworth, Martin (ed.), *The Survival of Poetry*, Faber, 1970.

Tomlinson, Charles, 'The Middlebrow Muse', *Essays in Criticism*, VII, January 1957, pp. 208–17. Hostile view of Larkin's work.

Wain, John, 'Engagement or Withdrawal: Some Notes on the work of Philip Larkin', *Critical Quarterly*, VI, Summer 1964, pp. 167–78. Sensitive appreciation of Larkin's work.

Wain, John, 'English Poetry: The Immediate Situation', *Sewanee Review*, LXV, Summer 1957, pp. 353–74 on *The North Ship* and *The Less Deceived*.

Watson, J. R., 'The Other Larkin', *Critical Quarterly*, Vol. 17, No. 4, Winter 1975, pp. 347–60. Argues for Larkin's 'seriousness' in non-religious context.

Other Books of Interest

CHAMBERS, HARRY, (ed.), *An Enormous Yes: In Memoriam Philip Larkin*, Peterloo, 1987.

DAVIE, DONALD, *Thomas Hardy and British Poetry*, Routledge & Kegan Paul, 1972.

HARTLEY, GEORGE, (ed.), Listen. A Tribute to Philip Larkin, Marvell Press, 1987.

MORRISON, BLAKE, *The Movement: British Poetry and fiction of the 1950s*, Oxford University Press, 1980.

PRESS, JOHN, *Rule and Energy*, Oxford University Press, 1963.

PRESS, JOHN, *A Map of Modern English Verse*, Oxford University Press, 1969.

THWAITE, ANTHONY (ed.), *Larkin At Sixty*, Faber, 1982. Interesting collection of memoirs, anecdotes and criticism collected for Larkin's sixtieth birthday.

THWAITE, ANTHONY, *Poetry Today. A Critical Guide to British Poetry 1960–1984*, Longman, 1985.

At the time of writing (1987), the official biography by Andrew Motion is in preparation.

Larkin Reading his Verse

The Less Deceived on disc, Marvell Press, LPVI, and cassette, Marvell Press Listen Cassettes.

The Whitsun Weddings, with introductory comments by the poet available on disc, Marvell Press LPV6, and cassette, Marvell Press Listen Cassettes.

High Windows, available on disc, Argo Records.

On Record, a selection of seven poems available on disc, Yorkshire Arts Association YA3(B).

The Poet Speaks, a selection of five poems with introductory comments by the poet available on disc, Argo Record Company, PLP 1088, Record Eight.

Interviews with Larkin

'Four Young Poets – I: Philip Larkin', *Times Educational Supplement*, 13 July 1956, p. 993.

'Speaking of Writing XIII: Philip Larkin', *The Times*, 20 February 1964, p. 16.

'Four Conversations', talking to Ian Hamilton, *London Magazine*, Vol. IV, No. 6, November 1964.

'The Unsung Gold Medallist', Philip Oakes' sketch of Larkin's lifestyle and family background, *Sunday Times Magazine*, 27 March 1966.

'A Conversation with Philip Larkin', *Tracks*, 1, Summer 1967.

'A Poet on the 8.15', *The Guardian*, 20 May 1965, Interview with John Horder, p. 9.

'A Sharp-Edged View', *Times Educational Supplement*, 19 May 1972, p. 19. Interviewed by Frances Hill.

'Raymond Gardner interviews Dr Larkin about his approach to life and poetry', *The Guardian*, 31 March 1973, p. 12.

'A Great Parade of Single Poems: Interview with Anthony Thwaite', *The Listener*, 12 April 1973, pp. 472–3.

'Profile 3. Philip Larkin', *The New Review, Vol. I, No. 3, pp. 25–9*.

'A Voice for our Time', *The Observer*, 16 December 1979, p. 35. Interviewed by Miriam Gross. (Reprinted in *Required Writing*.)

Viewpoints: Poets in Conversation, Haffenden, John (ed.), Faber, 1982.

'An Interview with *Paris Review*', *Paris Review*, No. 84, 1982, pp. 45–72. (Reprinted in *Required Writing*.)

Index